# TABLE OF CONTENTS

# PHOTO CREDITS

# Acknowledgments

My first and most heart-felt thanks must go to the person without whom this work could not have been created: Daria Zeilinger. She has been more than just a sponsor of this book and a virtual sister to me personally. She has been the living memory of my father, Edward C. Harwood, since his death in 1980. She was one of the few people who knew him best and who felt that his goals were valuable enough to spend a good part of her life fulfilling his memory.

Another such person is my brother Fred. He and his faithful wife Michelle gave all their adult energies to my father, while somehow managing to raise two great kids in the process. Their suggestions and support for this book have been invaluable. Fred is also an excellent photographer and supplied some of the images.

My brother Bill also devoted hours reading my draft and writing comments that have been most useful. My sister Midge supplied the accurate time-frame foundations that started me off on my way through many files of archives.

Professor Steven R. Cunningham, former Chief Economist at the American Institute for Economic Research, has made some useful suggestions for which I am grateful. Thanks are also due to AIER's editors, Marcia Stamell, Lynndee Kemmet and Sarah Todd, who helped me prepare the preliminary drafts.

I cannot begin to name all of those who stood by my father during his lifetime, all the more so since a few financial contributors were nameless at the time. But in the hopes that you know who you are, I thank you for helping him realize his goals.

Finally, I thank my husband who put his life on hold for five years while I banged away on the computer at home and at the AIER archives. Without his patience and generosity, this work would not exist.

Edward C. Harwood, circa 1931
*"For integrity there is no substitute."*

# Chapter 1

The harsh words of the interoffice memo confounded him. If there was one thing young Capt. Edward C. Harwood had never feared it was authority, but this missive was the latest in a long series of menacing harangues that came from the brass hats in Washington. They did not agree with his interpretation of the Army officer's mission.

Upon graduating from West Point at the end of World War I, he had sworn as an officer to "support and defend the Constitution of the United States against all enemies, foreign and domestic." The wording of this oath implied a conscientious and primary allegiance to the principles embodied in the founding document, and only secondarily to any superior officers or the sitting president, who were themselves subservient to the U.S. Constitution.

In 1933 after President Roosevelt's first few months, Harwood had concluded that some of the administration's policy recommendations were damaging to basic constitutional principles. In deference to his sworn oath, and in spite of his professional military duty of allegiance to the commander in chief, Harwood chose to step outside his role as an Army officer by speaking in public about his opinions (dressed in civilian clothes) and even publishing articles.

The Washington hierarchy did not approve. As expressed by one of their representatives, Brig. Gen. G.B. Pillsbury, chief of engineers, the young captain had a "complete misconception of the duties and responsibilities of an officer of the Army of the United States." Harwood was a commissioned soldier and therefore must place himself at the mercy of his superior officers and of the president of the United States no matter what the inconvenience or dangers involved. He must not attempt to split himself into "two personalities" in an effort to skirt this military obligation.

> He must abstain from political discussions of any kind. Since
> economics and politics are closely interwoven, his writings on
> economics, so long as he remains an officer, must be strictly curtailed.[2]

Almost from the start of Harwood's outspokenness, Army agents had begun investigating this embarrassing exercise of free speech on the part of one of their own. Some held him in contempt, but others were surprisingly sympathetic. On one occasion an inspector came to Harwood's MIT office and sat down opposite him at the desk. The fellow took out one of Harwood's articles and placed it in such a way that Harwood could read the marginal notes. Portions of printed text were underlined and the handwriting read: "Investigate and stop this—Lauchlin Currie, The White House." Currie was a former Harvard professor of economics who had become one of Roosevelt's close economic advisors. Obviously, at least some of the War Department's prodding was initiated from higher up.

As the object of multiple investigations by the War Department over a period of several years, Harwood had plenty of opportunity to reflect long and hard on the issue. In the beginning, his bold replies laid out his understanding of the officer's oath. He argued, for example, that:

> The effective application of [your] policy in the past would probably
> have resulted in the removal from the Army of several of its most
> illustrious officers (Washington, Grant, Sherman, Scott, and others)

and would effectively stop the publication of much material by officers now living....[3]

The generals responded to each of his defenses with warnings but offered few counterarguments. Perhaps they felt their authoritative opinion should suffice, which was a superior attitude that would have irritated Harwood all the more. But the latest missive he held in his hand was the strongest to date and an obvious attempt to terminate the debate once and for all. It ended with this:

> The Chief of Engineers appreciates the ability and talent of Captain Harwood and will be gratified to have him remain an officer of the Corps of Engineers. If, however, Captain Harwood is unwilling to fulfill the entire duty and responsibility of a commissioned officer, relinquishing all rights and privileges of a private citizen inconsistent therewith, he should forthwith submit a request that his resignation be accepted. [4]

What had begun as a series of reprimands had now morphed into an ultimatum. Harwood's choices were clear to his conscience but impossible to accept. The powerful Washington hierarchy had given him only two alternatives: either conform and shut up, or continue to spout off after retiring from the Army at the early age of 35 with no pension and six mouths to feed. Leaving the Army would mean the curtailment of a career, which in itself would not be a hardship. Harwood actually relished the idea of turning his full attention to the small economic research institute he had founded two years before, but he also recognized the financial impossibility.

He would have to find a way to stay put, at least for the time being, while removing any signs of impropriety. Yet he would not —could not—admit that a military officer had to renounce his private civil rights. President Roosevelt, whether well-intended or ill-advised, was steering the country into a New Deal that would endanger the principles for which George Washington, Thomas Jefferson, Samuel Adams and James Madison had risked their lives. Harwood could not remain silent and still call himself a man of honor. As ironic as it seemed and contrary to his oath, he was not going to be allowed to defend the Constitution while in the Army.

He drafted and redrafted another long memo to the War Department to point out its folly. Had not many of history's dictators relied on the compliance of silent subordinate officers to overthrow the basic human rights of their subjects? But Harwood never sent that memo. Perhaps Col. John J. Kingman, his friend, defender and immediate supervisor, advised him against it; or maybe he came to see the futility.

Harwood managed to keep a low profile for a couple of years leading up to 1937. He continued to publish his thoughts but did so under the cover of his associates at the research institute. Then through a quirk of circumstance, the Army passed a new rule allowing officers to retire with a pension after only eighteen and a half years of service. The offer was intended to encourage the higher-ranking soldiers to move off the active payroll, but its effect was just the opposite as many younger men took advantage of the deal. Realizing its error, the Army soon retired the rule but by that time Harwood had seized the opportunity. He had been granted a way out of his predicament.

He coordinated his departure date with some accumulated leave to give himself plenty of time to get organized, and he officially retired by January 1938. The financial relief lifted the much heavier weight of moral defeat from his shoulders. With a modest pension to tide him over the difficult transition period, Harwood was now certain that he would make something of his little research institute.

∗     ∗     ∗     ∗     ∗

Harwood's secondary vocations as an economist and financial advisor had begun as a hobby during his early Army career. What had initially been curiosity turned into fascination as his knowledge expanded. By the early age of 27, while still an Army officer studying only in his spare time and well before he had attracted the attention of the War Department, his scholarly writings had begun to find publishers. The first came out on his birthday, October 28, 1927, in *The Annalist*, a weekly owned by The New York Times Company. Others soon appeared in *Barron's*, *Wall Street Magazine* and similar financial periodicals. Just months before the beginning of the Great Depression, several of his articles described an imminent and violent market correction. For example, on August 2, 1929, he wrote in *The Annalist*:

> [T]he time may not be far distant when the country will realize, in the light of a cold gray "morning after," that it has just been on another credit-splurging spree.[5]

None of the so-called Keynesian economists had seen it coming —not even the great John Maynard Keynes himself, who lost a good portion of his savings in the crash.

Three years later, in 1932 after having prepared a master's thesis based on banking statistics, Harwood wrote his first book setting forth his analysis of the problems underlying the crisis. In 1933, with the encouragement of influential businessmen and professional friends who had studied his book, he created the research entity and called it the American Institute for Economic Research. Its purpose was to find more useful solutions to economic problems than those proposed by academia. By definition, some of his findings and published commentary involved public policy, and so it was during these years that the War Department investigations had begun.

Through his studies of economics, Harwood came to the conclusion that the science was not yet ripe to play the role certain politicians and economists had thrust upon it. His personal approach allowed only more modest expectations through the use of statistics, logical analysis, observation and verification. He proceeded from the assumption that, in spite of the inherent limitations imposed by the subject matter, some economic events could be observed and hypotheses advanced if one used the proper methodology; but that to go too far was folly.

He found two areas where his research allowed him to draw workable hypotheses. The first concerns the evolution of the idea of freedom as embodied best by the U.S. Constitution and by the progress it has brought to western civilization, especially in the United States. The second hypothesis lay in the field of money credit aspects of the business cycle.

*First Hypothesis: Greater protection of freedom in the United States has helped increase the standard of living of Americans.*

Harwood theorized that the tremendous advance in the standard of living of most Americans was due to our social economic system, which affords a maximum of freedoms protected by the U.S. Constitution. Our wise Founding Fathers based this set of societal rules on their astute study of the evolution of human rights from ancient Greece through the Magna Carta, and they sought to protect these rights from the recurring tendency of governments to become tyrannical.

Harwood found that limitations upon government are essential to maintaining a maximum of freedom and to continuing the evolution of our standard of living. Excess government influence and power tend to corrupt market processes by suppressing fair competition, creating incentives for lobbying and "lawyering up," attracting unscrupulous individuals to the ranks of the powerful in both the public and private sectors, and fostering an unholy alliance between politicians and special interest groups.

*Second Hypothesis: Harwood's Statistical Analysis of Money-Credit Aspects of the Business Cycle*

Harwood believed that relative monetary stability is another major factor contributing to the rapid advancement of the western world's standard of living during the 19th century. He saw that a highly evolved and private system of money creation and standardization had kept the money supply on a relatively even keel over the long term, both in America before the turn of the 20th century and in Europe for over a hundred years.

Harwood theorized that this stability was furnished by the interaction of two elements, the gold standard and sound commercial banking (more about these in subsequent chapters). However, he noted that since the late 19th century money had come under increasing political control. This more centralized control of the money supply had not kept it stable, on the contrary.

Through his statistical studies, Harwood noted periods of rapid inflating of the money supply, especially during World War I and thereafter. He believed this was the cause of the increasing breadth and depth of the business cycle during those years. The inflating caused a misallocation of capital by augmenting speculative profits during boom periods, and then it amplified losses during the subsequent inevitable deflationary bust periods and spread the misery to the general population.

With the insertion of political will into the money-creation process, businesses and the public were forced to deal with a new factor in their life: unpredictable future monetary policy decisions. The inflating and subsequent deflating caused distortions in market pricing signals, interest and exchange rates, bank credit availability and the purchasing power of the monetary unit itself.

Harwood noted that a policy of inflating the money supply inhibited the workings of the gold standard and encouraged the disregard of sound banking principles. He felt that these conditions during the second decade of the 20th century were probably the proximate causes of the crises that occurred soon thereafter. Yet such a policy of inflating was condoned by politicians and other agents who had risen to positions of influence during the inflationary years. The justifications for it came from the findings of reputed economists whose work Harwood found to be deficient.

Harwood was not alone in reaching these conclusions. Other thinkers, including Henry George, Henry Hazlitt and Friedrich von Hayek, also perceived the value of the gold standard and the dangers of state intervention. They, too, recognized and fought the seizure of monetary control by governmental entities. But unlike these great thinkers who tended to abstain from direct criticism of their colleagues, the outspoken Harwood dared to expose the fallacies of well-known academics whose untested theories he believed were being used by politicians to validate the adoption of harmful monetary policy.

\*     \*     \*     \*     \*

Thus, Harwood felt that government-created central banking was probably the source of some of the problems he observed. The Federal Reserve System's creation in 1913 resulted from the desire of legislators in the early part of the 20th century to assuage the fluctuations of the business cycle, provide clearing-house tools to the banking industry and win the upcoming war through the extension of credit. Although Harwood could hardly blame Congress for having these ambitions, he felt that government control of the money supply facilitated serious monetary mischief through multiple unintended consequences.

In 1933, after only 20 years of the Fed's existence, the dollar had become so irredeemably inflated that Roosevelt decided to devalue it outright. To Harwood, such official sanctification of the dollar's weakness condoned almost two decades of chronic and treasonous theft from the pockets of America's working and saving population. He called it "legalized embezzlement."

The devaluation and the conditions that led up to it were some of the problems of which Harwood chose to speak and write when he was a young Army captain. As he watched what he thought was a man-made tragedy taking place before his eyes, he vowed to spend the rest of his life warning people about the effects of their government's public-policy choices on their standard of living. He defended the publics right to carry on everyday market transactions with a stable currency, and he argued that Congress was not living up to its constitutional duty to oversee the maintenance of the dollar's value.

As the years passed, he began to give specific and innovative investment notions to a few investors in order to help at least some Americans preserve the purchasing power of their savings. Harwood's investment followers became the testing ground for his understanding of economics, financial markets and the macro events that influence them. He liked to say that the results of his advice would put his analysis to the test, much like agricultural colleges used private farms to try out new seeds and animal husbandry techniques. Looking back, the outcome was a uniquely positive investment record.

A few examples: Harwood foresaw the enormous business boom that began after World War II, and he steered investors into the U.S. stock market to reap large profits. Starting in 1958, the advisory group he created at his institute began recommending gold-related assets in reaction to the huge inflationary forces then in play. He realized that at some point the standardized dollar-gold parity would have to give way to the tremendous pressure building up from chronic monetary inflating, just as had happened in the 1920's.

In the late 1960's and early 1970's, as pressure from chronic inflating increased all the more, he began advising investors to put all disposable income into permitted gold coins, gold related stocks and foreign assets. He stayed the course against many odds, some of which are described in this book. Gold peaked in 1980, the year of his death. Although the road was rocky, most of the wiser investors came out way ahead of the game.

✳     ✳     ✳     ✳     ✳

Harwood was a man of contrasts: driven, demanding and relentless, yet at times gentle, generous and forgiving. He could often be dead serious but just as frequently revealed a good sense of humor. He was as rigorous and upright as he was full of common sense, wit and creativity. Friends described him as a hero, a genius, a word-smith, a maverick, a man of "tremendous presence" and impeccable integrity, but also as "headstrong, controversial and downright ornery."[6]

Someone once asked Albert Einstein what should be taught in school. The learned physicist replied, "In teaching history, such personalities should be discussed extensively, who benefited mankind through independence of character and judgment."[7] Edward C. Harwood was certainly one of these.

# Chapter 2: Formative Years

*Tall oaks from little acorns grow.*[8]

Edward Crosby Harwood once remarked that his forebearers might have been gold beaters, those artisans who turn small nuggets of gold into many square feet of decorative gold leaf. He may have been joking, but if it were true it certainly would have been appropriate.

Although an amateur search in Britain by his widow did find some likely candidates, none were gold beaters. She found the Harwood name carved on numerous centuries-old tombstones, some of which were in the County of Lincolnshire, England. One ancestor, a Sir Edward Harwood, was born of farmers in 1597 in the town of Thurlby. He served in the military under King Charles I, rose to the rank of colonel, was killed in battle at the age of 35 and was buried in The Hague, Holland. Another namesake was an 18th century English doctor of divinity who authored a controversial vernacular translation of the New Testament. It had little success, but his legacy earned him a short page in Wikipedia.

There may be more Harwood ancestors of interest, but most important is Harwood's father, reportedly the sixth generation of eldest-son Edwards. He came to America in a ship from England when he was just a boy. He grew up in Massachusetts, married the daughter of a successful grocer and became the archetypical Forgotten Man.

"Pops" Harwood was a jack-of-all-trades who worked at whatever occupation he could find to feed his family and to finance the whims of a spendthrift wife. When his son Eddie, the second of four children, was born on October 28, 1900, Edward Sr. reported his profession as a trunk salesman. When Eddie graduated from high school 17 years later, father was working as an executive in the power department of the Fisk Rubber Company in Chicopee Falls, Mass. Before two more years had passed, he had changed employers several times and settled into a job at a bakery. Like so many, he was hard working, paid all his taxes and seldom complained.

Although this humble man never achieved great wealth, he was probably the only person his son ever revered. As a teenager, Edward Jr. wrote a letter to his mother stating that, in spite of his father's modest achievements, he considered him "the most successful man" he had ever met, the kind of person who had "those qualities without which money would be useless and with which money is unnecessary." Father had "the physical, mental and moral man completely under control."

> To know him is to respect, love, and honor him. I have never heard anyone speak other than good of him. To do so would be absurd on the face of it. [9]

Judging from these words and from his family's modest circumstances, one can understand the origin of the younger Edward's heart-felt respect for all those ordinary citizens who work hard and mind their own business. But nothing about his background foretold of the intimate relationship he would cultivate with Lady Liberty and her guardian angel, Gold.

✳     ✳     ✳     ✳     ✳

Harwood spent his uneventful adolescence in the modest suburbs of Springfield, Mass. during the bustling beginnings of the 20th century. The only attributes that might have distinguished him from other children were his great brown eyes, his intense energy, a tendency to blush and a precocious sense of a good investment. As an adolescent, he accumulated some savings by distributing newspapers and cleaning out neighbors' basements. The Curtis Publishing Company, a large magazine distributor of the day, held a competition for the highest sales of one of their periodicals. Eddie was about 12 or 13 at the time and saw the prize money as an opportunity to get a head start on his college tuition at "Aggie," the agricultural college nearby. He thought up a strategy: he would buy up a maximum of the magazines with his own cash and then throw them into the dump down by the Connecticut River. The ruse worked and he won the prize, even if moral justice lost out. The latter got her

revenge, however, when his mother "borrowed" his savings for a down payment on a house.

In Technical High School, young Harwood's exceptional scholastic achievements, quiet charm and conspicuous debating talent brought him to the fore. By the time he graduated in June of 1918, he had been elected class president, "Most Popular Boy," "Best All-Around Boy" and "Handsomest Boy." He was about to prepare for admission to "Aggie" when a stroke of luck resulted in the opportunity for an engineering education at the U.S. Military Academy at West Point. Massachusetts Congressman Gillette's first two choices could not attend the Academy because of failed exams. The school district then turned to Harwood. Instead of a country farmer, he became a military cadet right in the middle of the greatest war the world had ever known.

The 17-year-old was transformed by the experience, as were many of his age. All the cadets aspired to be sent to the front in France. The depleted U.S. Army needed officers. Harwood wrote home about the deafening howls of elation that shook the mess hall windowpanes when the superintendent announced everyone would be graduating early to go off to war. A few months later, in November 1918, he described the despondent silence when they learned of the armistice.

His class still graduated after only two years, but it had to forgo a summer vacation. West Point's rigorous structure taught Harwood self-discipline, the honor code, teamwork and proper study habits. Week by week, he went up in the published rankings. He ended his military schooling at the age of 19, having earned sixth place in academics, 10th overall and the honorary title of distinguished cadet.

All the young men who made it through to graduation came away with a newfound maturity and a bearing like a flag pole. Engraved in their heart was the West Point motto: duty—honor— country. With a Bachelor of Science degree in hand, Harwood took his oath as an officer of the Army to defend the U.S. Constitution against all enemies, foreign and domestic. Then he went on to further studies in civil engineering at Rensselaer Polytechnic Institute.

After two more years spent obtaining his full engineering degree in June of 1922, he married his childhood sweetheart, Harriet. She was the young lady who sat kitty-corner from him in grade school; in whose home he had played chaperoned games of hide and seek; on whose doorstep he had paused before knocking in order to catch a bit more of her piano playing and singing; and who had received mournful letters from the lonely cadet several times a week.

On the way back from the countryside jaunt that they called their honeymoon, they stopped off at West Point to reminisce about the few dates they had there. It was Saturday dance night. He, or she, had a crazy idea for a last-fling goodbye to their irresponsible youth. He ran up to the dormitory room of a couple of unknown cadets. The men jumped up at attention and saluted. Harwood asked one of them to fetch a dress uniform, which he donned. He returned to an admiring Harriet and they sauntered over to the dance hall to relive their first romantic moments.

They danced together and then wandered out onto the balcony to look at the moon over the Hudson River. After a few delicious moments he got a tap on the shoulder. The young cadets had informed a supervisory officer, who was now asking Harwood and Harriet to leave the premises immediately. They left, somewhat embarrassed but no less tickled by the experience. Harwood stopped off at the West Point superintendent's office the next morning to offer his name, and then the two left for his new station in North Carolina.

He had almost forgotten the incident when, one month later, he received a notice to report to West Point for temporary duty. As soon as he got there, an officer served him with court-martial papers. After an anxious day or two, he was assigned a military attorney who decided that, given his client's youth, disarming charm and fine record, Harwood should tell his own story during the trial. He did so with simple and honest words, painting a vivid picture of the innocent newlyweds they were. The confounded judges, after pressing him with questions, decided that military rigor required some sort of punishment, so they stripped him of a grade for impersonating a cadet.

Harwood earned back his rank of first lieutenant during the next four years at Army bases in North Carolina. His rote military engineering duties included a quick-study apprenticeship in the management of raw Army recruits, one of whom was responsible for breaking Harwood's right molar. After a year or so of similar challenges to his innate abundance of confidence, Harwood was ultimately able to tame the men by demonstrating his good horsemanship, his leadership ability and his fine-tuned sense of fairness. His men were so won over that they bought him an Elgin watch as a gift at the end of their term together. He recognized that such a gesture was rare. The watch took its place among his prized possessions and stayed there until the end of his life.

Daughter Marjorie arrived in 1924. Harwood and Harriet's bland but pleasant family life was peppered with bridge games, horseback jaunts through the pine-covered countryside and visits to the folks in Springfield. Harwood once remarked that bored peacetime Army officers often were tempted to drink, gamble or chase women, but that his own natural instincts seemed only to lead him to spend an inordinate amount of time at the library. This was where he began to study the works of economists, philosophers and the

U.S. founding fathers. In his mid-20's, Harwood discovered his passion for economics, finance, scientific methodology and America's constitutional principles.

*Historical Perspective: Monetary Policy of the Times*

In the early 20th century, developed nations based their monetary policy on the gold standard coupled with what Harwood considered to be a sound commercial banking system. The gold standard provided a means of assuring the stability of the monetary unit's purchasing power. In 1900, one dollar was set to be exchangeable at any time for 1/20.67th of a troy ounce of gold. Otherwise stated, one could procure one troy ounce of gold at any bank for $20.67.

The sound commercial banking system of those days, partnered with the gold standard, furnished a reliable source of money supply, or what Harwood preferred to call purchasing media. Gold coins and gold certificates were prevalent at the time, but the amount of world gold production was limited (as it still is), and so the free market had evolved an effective means of creating temporary purchasing media to cover market transactions. The result was that the total purchasing media in circulation equaled gold and silver coins, gold and silver certificates, bank accounts representing gold reserves and also bank certificates and accounts representing the precise value of products and services coming to market, plus any savings.[*] A second thing that the sound commercial banking system provided was a relatively safe method of lending and borrowing. These were both limited by the stock of the nation's savings, by the risk-taking acumen of independent bankers and by each banker's individual liability.

---

*More on this in Chapter 4. For information about how this system worked, consult two books Harwood recommended: *Money and Banking*, by Professor Frederick A. Bradford, and *The Theory and History of Banking*, by Professor Charles F. Dunbar.

Overexpansion of bank credit did occur, but it could, and often was, chastised by bank failures. The economy's ups and downs followed the normal tide swings of the natural business cycle. Harwood and others realized that absolute control of the business cycle is neither attainable, nor desirable. As Joseph Schumpeter's phrase "creative destruction" implies, capitalism requires that less healthy business models fail and make way for the stronger ones. The phenomenon tends to occur in waves. The failures are as important a part of the process as the successes.

Creative destruction doesn't always have to destroy to be effective. The mere apprehension of loss can motivate behavior modification. For example, fear of bank failures such as those that occurred during the 19th century very probably rendered bankers more cautious than they would otherwise have been, leading to frequent and shallow cycles and a relatively resilient local economy. On the other hand, Harwood observed some pretty fearless credit creation by certain bankers during the 1920's, and he believed it was one of the proximate causes of the subsequent great wave of weakness in the economy. Again, starting in the 1950's, Harwood predicted that a similar long wave of exaggerated expansion would lead to a deep and lasting crisis, which it certainly did in the late 1970's. A third large wave seems to have taken place from the 1990's until 2007.

Harwood found that fiat monetary systems, i.e. those that do not abide by a monetary anchor such as the gold standard, tend to experience exacerbated and extended booms and busts precisely because they lack the naturally limiting monetary parameter the anchor provides. Each time governments have drifted away from standardization or have purposely tried such fiat systems, the monetary unit has depreciated almost to zero, often contributing to social disorder. Without a respected standard and without healthy banking customs, bankers and money managers may perceive no early warning system, may have little fear of the repercussions of poor decisions and/or may not be forced to retract the overexpansion before the situation becomes critical.

*Public Policy Perspective of Harwood's Times*

By the beginning of the 20th century, the debate about the optimum degree of government centralization was in full swing. Populist legislators came into the majority feeling confident that they could improve the state of the union by increasing the powers of government. (This is not so much a political issue as it is a public policy issue; note that there are big government Democrats and big government Republicans. The terms politics and public policy are often used interchangeably. For the purposes of this book, the author uses politics in the sense of party politics, and public policy to refer to a set of plans of action, or inaction, affecting the public.)

The pre-World War I Congress, like many wartime legislatures before it, was well aware of the short-term benefits of creating credit to finance military expenses. The individuals chosen to run the new Federal Reserve System created in 1913 were banking professionals and economic academics who believed a central bank can inflate the currency, provide as much credit as needed and then retract it at will. According to Harwood, at the end of the war in 1918 and after the first "successful" round of inflating, the Federal Reserve did try to retract the extra credit. The result was a recession that lasted until 1921. Perhaps for political reasons the central bankers decided to mitigate the pain by allowing the monetary expansion to remain in circulation and even to grow.

The subsequent expansion they created was much larger and less localized than had occurred under a less centralized banking system. Therefore, the repercussions were more widely felt and lasted longer. The inflating became a national phenomenon with no particular individual banks shouldering the blame. Essentially, the buck had been transferred from private bankers answering to each's own market sector, to the central bankers who answered to no one except those individuals who had appointed them to office. Incentives became skewed. The creation of the Fed had now given banks the opportunity to allow the inflating to continue unabated and to create an even bigger maladjustment. This, according to Harwood, is what happened during the 1920's leading up to the 1929 crisis, and he confirmed this by a thorough study of banking statistics.

*Harwood's Personal Initiation into the World of Finance*

Under these circumstances, credit and its alter ego, debt, expanded during these nine years. This was true even on a consumer level as lay-away purchasing became more and more popular and less and less selective. During the first part of the booming 1920's, Harwood was at a North Carolina Army station. At mid-decade, he was transferred to the Territory of Hawaii for four years. The base on the island also had a fantastic library where he continued to fill his head with economics, finance, the philosophy of science and scientific methodology. It was also during this time that Harwood—still rather brash and full of himself—jumped head first into the role of investment advisor.

His financial studies had rendered him well-versed in all of the brokers' tools of the trade: puts, calls, buying and selling short or long, betting on margin, stop losses. The boom was well along by 1926 and 1927. He already believed that a cyclical downturn of the stock market was a sure thing and that he could time it with his perfected knowledge. His confidence was as great as the profits he promised, which were between 10 and 20 percent a year. He persuaded about eight of his Army buddies to join him in a speculative venture.

The first successes encouraged them all to invest more of their rare extra cash. Soon each had put in hundreds of dollars, which would be the equivalent of thousands of dollars today. After a few months things began to turn sour. He asked for their patience and was such a good salesman that he got it. His luck came back, but then it disappeared again. His vision of a market collapse was ill timed. Somehow stocks just kept rising. Economist Keynes supposedly memorialized the conundrum with the famous comment that "the market can remain irrational longer than you can remain solvent."

After about a year of this, the funds were so low that Harwood gave up. In 1928 he wrote to his speculative colleagues:

> I feel that I have unintentionally misrepresented the possibilities in our adventure, through a lack of experience on my part. That being the case, I could not be satisfied to drop the project without seeing that your losses are returned to you.... No one must ever be able to say that he lost out through failure on my part, except myself. [10]

He wasn't obligated to refund their money. He had never guaranteed a profit, and all knew it was a speculative venture. But he sent his personal promissory note to each man and paid them all back within eight years.

Although no profits were earned and the downturn had yet to appear, Harwood's early experiences in the investment trenches were eye opening. First, he learned about hubris and humility. Second, he acquired a healthy, life-long skepticism of the brokerage business, realizing that it was the only sector he had enriched with his buying and selling. He started telling the joke about the broker who takes a friend to the local marina to see his luxurious yacht. The admirer is impressed and then turns to the broker and says, "Now show me the yachts of your clients."

### The Long-Awaited Crash Finally Arrives

Thus chastised, Harwood turned back to his study of economic history. His articles were beginning to find enthusiastic publishers. When his four-year stint in Hawaii came to an end, the War Department sent him back to RPI for further studies in accordance with his own request. (This was before the infamous investigations.) He obtained two master's degrees in 18 months, one in engineering and the other in business administration. At the same time, he continued to write articles for financial journals.

He already had a prodigious memory and was developing a keen analytical mind. For his business administration thesis, he did the extensive statistical research that later became the basis for his economic theories and for a tool he called the Harwood Index of Inflating, both of which he would expound upon later in his first book, *Cause and Control of the Business Cycle*.

By the late 1920's the chronic inflating of credit, with its resultant over-issuance of dollars, had spread overseas as a natural result of international trade. The U.S. balance-of-payments account was way out of kilter. Trading partners began to doubt the capacity of American banks to cover the imbalance. They started demanding gold, as was their due, and moved it out of the U.S. in shiploads. The U.S. central bankers, still claiming to abide by the gold standard, tried to rein in inflating by tightening monetary policy. Some say they did so too abruptly and too late.

The result was that in 1929 over-expanded credit finally collapsed all over the country, just as Harwood had predicted. Most people are familiar with the story: Florida real estate markets went bust; the New York stock market crashed; overleveraged Western farming communities imploded; people in the South couldn't eat while people in the North couldn't sell their crops. These were all signs of the misallocation of capital, which, according to Harwood, is a normal side effect of inflating.

The Great Depression and its aftermath exposed the budding economist to the ravages of a disintegrating political and monetary system. The central bankers thought price deflation had run its course by 1931, and so they tried once again to retract excessive credit. However, prices dropped even lower. Debtors, especially the farmers representing a good portion of the public, were stretched to the breaking point. A desperate Congress under Hoover had already passed what some legislators thought were palliative measures such as the Smoot-Hawley tariffs, and by 1932 the politicians were debating the Goldsborough Bill, a piece of legislation that would have given the Federal Reserve the power to change the gold exchange value of the dollar. As soon as the hint of official dollar devaluation hit the table, the public and America's international creditors panicked.

Roosevelt's campaign platform was very different from the policies he ultimately implemented. According to Roosevelt's own Fed Governor Marriner Eccles, Hoover and Roosevelt gave "speeches [that] often read like a giant misprint, in which Roosevelt and Hoover speak each other's lines."[11] In his campaigning, Roosevelt called for a 25-percent reduction of public expenditures, a balanced budget and a sound currency backed by gold. But once elected, he proceeded to implement just the opposite.

After Roosevelt's inauguration, people began pulling money out of the banks as fast as they could. The high number of bank failures led Roosevelt to close them all for a few days. Roosevelt then did what Harwood thought no president would ever dare to do: he issued executive orders declaring a state of emergency and making possession of gold illegal, a move that would allow him to devalue the dollar and retain the profits for the U.S. Treasury.

Harwood's heart must have sunk as he learned of Roosevelt's plans, and he began to realize that the U.S. Constitution's most lethal enemies could indeed be domestic. Not only did Roosevelt make the campaign promise to defend the gold standard and then renege on it as soon as he took office in 1933, but he also denied people the basic property right even to possess the metal. Unaware of the later repercussions to his career, Harwood tore the president's big-government policies apart at every opportunity.

Congress confirmed the devaluation with the Gold Reserve Act of 1934. It was done to relieve the pressure on debtors, creditors be damned.

Creditors were not only the foreign nations holding U.S. dollar claims. They were also those people who had savings and widows with fixed pensions as yet unprotected by any CPI adjustments. They were individual landlords with long-term binding lease contracts. They were the savers who had put their extra funds into gold coins that the government confiscated before the devaluation.

For all of these people, their "good-as-gold" dollars were replaced by devalued paper promises, and their credits, income and/or savings were cut almost in half. The administration hoped that this manipulation would save the debtors and permit the country to survive the crisis. America would be able to start afresh with its new dollar-gold exchange value revised to 1/35th of an ounce of gold.

According to Harwood, many factors contributed to the subsequent business cycle gyrations and relative stagnation up until World War II. Among these were the extent of the preceding inflationary boom with its excessive accumulation of debt; the tariffs; our reneging on the dollar; the New Deal and its wasteful "stimulus" spending; and the great burden on businesses posed by Roosevelt's multitude of new federal agencies such as the Interstate Commerce Commission, the National Recovery Administration, the Social Security Administration and the Securities and Exchange Commission.

By 1932, Harwood had been appointed Assistant Professor of Military Science and Tactics at the Massachusetts Institute of Technology in Cambridge, Massachusetts. He would soon direct the engineering operations for the widening of the Cape Cod Canal. He also began devoting every spare minute to his civilian research, article writing and speaking engagements on economics and public policy. When he published his first book based on his master's degree thesis, the work was successful enough to be recommended by the Book-of-the-Month Club. It precipitated correspondence from many businesspeople, as well as from a few academics.  Two of these, one at Dartmouth and one at Stanford, adopted the book for their university courses.

Harwood had found his niche: the defense of the common American citizen from the effects of bad policy and poor economic science.  He had no idea that it would put an early end to his military career, as it did in January of 1938; but he often remarked that life's troubles are like coins.  They have two sides: on one is strife; on the other is opportunity.

# Chapter 3: The Research Institute

*When words, or terms including names, no longer meant what they had been intended to mean, they lost their value.... Then men could not distinguish the truth from falsity, their consciences were blurred, they lost their sense of shame, and they abandoned virtue and adopted vicious courses.* – Attributed to Confucius[12]


Harwood had watched the Great Depression unfold throughout the early 1930's. He concluded that the worst of it was ultimately the result of a huge failed laboratory experiment in economic centralism backed by the work of an important faction of the academic community. Harwood counted among these Irving Fisher, the founder of monetarism who later developed a debt-deflation explanation for the Great Depression. Also on Harwood's list was John Maynard Keynes, the renowned English professor of economics at Kings College, Cambridge University.

Keynes's deficit-spending cures for the lack of consumption inspired first a private and then a public debate with Harwood. Harwood felt some of the scientific analysis used by Keynes was faulty, and in spite of the professor's authoritative reputation, Harwood pulled no punches. The ideas of Keynes, however, fit the centralist public policy chosen by Roosevelt's advisory team, and policies based upon them were indeed implemented. (In all fairness to Keynes, what is now known as Keynesian economics has little to do with his original ideas, which were far less radical. Keynes himself was well aware of the dangers of excessive monetary expansion, although he may have been a bit naïve about government's will to discipline itself.)

Early in 1933, Harwood's relationship with Harriet began to falter. By this time they had three children: Midge, Edward (the eighth and last generation of Edwards, nicknamed Ted and born in Hawaii) and little Richard. Harwood later confessed that they had married too young and were not as compatible as they had assumed. His heavy workload caused him to hire an attractive, impetuous secretary named Helen. He fell in love with her. Once he realized their feelings were mutual and that he could not mend his failing marriage, he told Harriet about the situation. He then put the house in Harriet's name, moved out and advised her to file for a no-contest divorce.

During his first year working with Helen, Harwood was still at MIT in his little ROTC office. A number of correspondents, all businessmen impressed with Harwood's book and economic theories, began discussing the idea of starting two organizations, one to study and one to promulgate their mutual economic policy recommendations. The principal proponents were Richard H. Somers, Alvan T. Simonds, Ralph E. Flanders, Ernest F. DuBrul and Sanford E. Thompson.

Harwood later credited a sixth man, Vannevar Bush, with giving him the final push to create an institute. Bush was a professor and dean of engineering as well as the vice-president of MIT. He later became a presidential science advisor and a strong proponent of the scientific method. It was he who came up with the idea of financing the proposed institute through public donations rather than through a few wealthy sources. This structure gave Harwood much-craved independence from any eventual ego or policy conflicts.

A few months after Helen arrived on the scene, and with the 1930's equivalent of about $3,000 in today's dollars, Harwood formed his small nonprofit economics research institute and named it the American Institute for Economic Research (AIER). As he phrased it himself in the institute's articles of association, his purpose in creating the entity was:

[T]o educate individual students and the general public, so that there may be more widespread understanding of the fundamental economic relationships affecting the citizens of the United States, both as individuals and as members of a complex economic society, with the ultimate object of advancing the welfare of the American people.[13]

He wanted to base all of the institute's work upon good and "useful" science. He maintained that in order to do this, scientists should adhere to the methodological precepts best described by two American philosophers, John Dewey and Arthur Bentley. Useful science starts with the formation of strong hypotheses based first and foremost on observation, analysis and statistics, which must then stand up to constant testing, peer review and revision. The process is continuous and never assumes that final truth exists. Dewey and Bentley also emphasized the importance of the use of clear and precise language, an idea to which Harwood fully subscribed.

The hard sciences of biology, physics and chemistry have made tremendous advances over the last few centuries due to this kind of methodology. However, because of the human aspects of the social, or behavioral sciences, progress in these has been slower. There are several reasons for this: the human social environment is hard to observe in a controlled laboratory setting. Also, we are studying ourselves; the observation process itself can influence the outcome; and human psychology, interaction and social arrangements are complex and subject to wide variation. In spite of these difficulties, the more scientific social scientists are making progress.

Harwood's ideas on methodology, drawn mainly from the work of Dewey and Bentley, were also influenced by the philosophers Charles S. Peirce, William James and Henry George. It was George's microeconomic and tax theory plus his thoughts on the use of language (but not his business cycle theory) that were of interest to Harwood. Harwood's economics also drew on the work of Gottfried von Haberler (his early work), Friedrich von Hayek (the monetary aspects), Ralph George Hawtrey, Henry Hazlitt and William Harold Hutt.

He was also influenced by the work of Carl Snyder, president of the American Statistical Association, and by Wesley C. Mitchell, one of the founders of the National Bureau of Economic Research. NBER was the first think tank to perform statistical and theoretical work in the U.S. Harwood felt that while these last two had achieved solid but modest success in using the tools of statistics, observation, a strict vocabulary and logic, they could have gone further in their analyses and benefited more fully from the results.

As a whole, however, Harwood was very disappointed by the poor state of economics as a science. He once wrote about it to a colleague in disparaging terms. Some influential theories were counterproductive, he felt, and he had a duty to inform the people of their misuse. He was frustrated by the fact that good work was ignored, while bad work was being allowed "to waste funds and jeopardize the Nation, indeed all of Western Civilization."[14]

He evaluated the most popular schools of thought of the day: The Austrian school, which relies on a theory called praxeology, obtained its principles properly from the use of analysis, statistics and observation, but also from generalized theoretical notions of human behavior that Harwood felt were sometimes inconclusive or simply convenient. Although some of Harwood's own theoretical conclusions were similar to those advanced by Austrian scientists such as Hayek, von Mises and others (indeed, Hayek was a good friend), they disagreed over details such as fractional reserve banking and the use of "real bills" (more about these shortly).

Harwood found that other schools of economics had too much confidence in the logical process itself and failed to notice that some of their underlying assumptions did not correspond to the evidence, or that their language use was inconsistent. A third group, the econometricians, seemed to be on the right track at first, but somewhere along the way they fell in love with the beauty of mathematical models to the detriment of scientific common sense. Harwood wrote that mathematics is a pleasing shorthand that can be a useful device to facilitate reasoning, but like pure logic it should in no event take the place of observation and verification.

Finally, Harwood found that the humility of his contemporaries was often trumped by their ambition, and that politicians were only too ready to take advantage of the resulting pseudoscientific bravado to justify their pet projects. Although some might fall into this trap, Harwood was determined not to make this mistake even if it meant forsaking a chance at the limelight. For example, he declined an invitation from Irving Fisher to participate in an elite panel of debate when he learned that a dissenting opinion would not be published. He thought this would give legislators the misleading impression that the advice was unanimous.

*     *     *     *     *

AIER grew rapidly right from the start. Yearly membership cost the dollar equivalent of one ounce of gold, which was $35 at the time. Today, this would be around $1,300. A handful of businesspeople were the first to give support, followed by an increasing number of members of the public. In return, they received a weekly information bulletin and intermittent special studies. Harwood hired the initial researchers and administrative staff for little money at the time. As Helen later remarked, during the Depression years there was no such thing as being too qualified for a job.

The weekly newsletter described market conditions in various sectors of the economy such as raw materials, the steel and auto industries, transportation, banking, and the stock and bond markets. Occasionally the updated Harwood Index of Inflating would appear. Researchers would also perform punctual studies of a particular industry such as the insurance business. Every bulletin would comment in lay person's language on current public-policy events that had an effect on the business and personal lives of readers.

Unlike some who claim to be impartial scientists and who refrain from any critique of public policy, Harwood did not hesitate to give his views on the decisions of politicians. He felt that his duty as a scientist included the revelation of *all* of his scientifically warranted findings including, first and foremost, that liberty is essential to objective and unbiased science. Without liberty of thought and expression, there can be no true science. (Remember that he would soon choose freedom of speech over a promising military career.)

Secondly, he declaimed to all who would listen that the exceptional economic wellbeing and comparatively high standard of living of Americans was the direct result of the application of the notions behind the U.S. Constitution. These notions—e.g., liberty, equality of opportunity, protection of property, equal justice before the law, and representative and constrained government—had found fertile ground in England before the Magna Carta and had been brought to America to flourish under a unique set of circumstances.

Harwood felt that property rights applied not only to land, buildings and other assets, but also to the product of one's work and to its unencumbered investment. As his investment-advisory experience matured, he began giving conservative but astute tips to the readers of the institute's bulletins. This aspect of the venture was so popular that he registered AIER with the SEC and took on the portfolios of a few supervisory clients. In time, this service became a wholly-owned subsidiary.

By 1938, the success of AIER was such that Harwood and Helen were able to buy a run-down building in Cambridge to house the growing institute. Real estate was still in the dumps, and Harwood persuaded the banker-owners that a regular income was better than a deteriorating loss on the books. The young couple and their employees worked together to fix up the accommodations with the little money available and with the help of Harwood's younger brothers, William and Harry.

Harwood was a popular speaker, and he and Helen were soon going on invitational grand tours by train all around the country. He spent the next five years addressing receptive audiences about the gold standard, sound commercial banking, limited government and the perils of inflating. Larger donors soon became interested in the institute's work. At the same time, knowing that inflating would continue unabated, Harwood got his investment followers into the stock market. He reasoned that another official devaluation of the dollar would probably occur but was not imminent, given that even Roosevelt seemed to be losing confidence in his powers to control the world. Harwood wrote:

> Never before in the history of this country have the over-privileged been offered better opportunities to secure speculative profits at the expense of their less well informed and less well-to-do fellow citizens. If this trend continues the masses of people will sink deeper in the mire of poverty, until in desperation leaders are chosen whose only qualification is a willingness to make reckless promises.[15]

His predictions of a business boom were accurate. For a number of years, those fortunate enough to have savings to invest were able to reap handsome profits. On the other hand, those living from day to day had to foot the bill with constant price increases. Harwood did his best to inform his readers of their options. Fortunately, the technological advances made in America and elsewhere were so great that the ensuing riches raised everyone's standard of living, at least for the time being.

Harwood and Helen were finally free to marry in October of 1938, after several years of Harwood's legal separation from Harriet as required by Massachusetts law. The institute's membership base, including the investors and charitable givers, continued to grow into the early 1940's. Then, observing the degradation of the international diplomatic situation, Harwood realized that America was going to join the Allies in the European and Pacific frays. He wrote to a former contact in Washington and reenlisted in the Army. He was initially sent back to MIT, but they soon found a post for him abroad. He said his goodbyes to his family, which now included two new little children, Bill and Eve. He went off on a ship to England to an undisclosed location that turned out to be London.

After a year and a half and several visits back home on military business, Harwood was transferred to Washington for what he thought was a permanent assignment. He and his new family settled into an old house in Virginia but were uprooted a few months later. Harwood was sent to the Tennessee wilderness for maneuvers. He spent a few weeks sleeping in a tent, playing war games, bathing only on rare occasions and becoming thoroughly frustrated with the outdated and rank-conscious working style of his crusty superiors. He was then assigned to join his friend and former Boston chief engineer, Pat Casey, in the Philippines.

Harwood lost 40 pounds while in the tropical jungles of Leyte and Luzon putting up with kamikaze bombers, knee-deep mud and a bad case of Malaria. Meanwhile, Helen took her two small toddlers to stay with her father in Florida. There, she gave birth to a third child, Fred. The institute bulletins continued to come out on schedule without her, written by the statistician Donald G. Ferguson and buttressed by pieces that Harwood managed to write in his quiet moments. He was able to keep abreast of the news, although with some tardiness. As he put it, war was "damn dirty, damn dull, and sometimes damn dangerous, but ... mostly just damn dull." [16]

Everyone in the family and immediate AIER community survived the war. Harwood advanced to the rank of colonel and retired again. He was awarded the Bronze Star on May 21, 1945, as well as the Legion of Merit. Feeling the need for some peace and quiet upon his return to Cambridge, he and Helen decided to pull up the whole operation and move it to the countryside, as they had plotted in their wartime letters. In one of the real estate brochures Helen had sent him was a dirt-cheap, overgrown, abandoned Cotswold-style manor house named Edgewood. It was situated in the beautiful Berkshire Hills of western Massachusetts. As soon as he got home they went to see it. After a few suspenseful negotiations with the Italian lumberman who owned the property, they signed on the dotted line and sold the smaller Boston building to Harvard for a good profit.

Edgewood as it looks today

Harwood by now had become "the Colonel" to his colleagues at AIER. The title stuck from then on, especially since he had begun wearing General MacArthur-style khakis around the office. With the staff still publishing in Cambridge near the end of 1945, Helen and the children began making the move to their new home in Great Barrington. Harwood and local workmen put the finishing touches on the main house, graded the land, laid water lines, plastered walls, hung doors, posed parquet floors and repainted. His skills in engineering, road-building, plumbing, outfitting and electrical work came in handy. With a little help from his two brothers and much admiration from little Billy and baby Freddy, the house was ready for occupancy by the Harwoods and about a dozen employees.

In 1946, the Harwoods began their new life and a year later came their fourth child, Katy, as a final afterthought. He was 47 and Helen was 42. In spite of the grandeur of the place, they furnished it according to their spartan tastes, complimenting its naked beauty and the peace of its surroundings. Helen had her hands full with the cooking and cleaning for four kids, a husband and a father-in-law.

They lost most of the Cambridge personnel who chose not to move to the countryside. However, Harwood had a knack for getting able people to join in his projects and he found replacements. He continued his writing and speaking. By this time his discourse had become fused with keen knowledgeable analysis and his strong sense of personal integrity. He was at his best in front of a group, with his West Point bearing, bright direct gaze, grounded self confidence, occasional sharp wit, incredible debating acumen and unlimited stock of original ideas.

Edgewood often received impromptu Sunday visitors. Harwood would give them the grand tour and answer questions about their personal financial affairs with no thought of remuneration. Whether or not they subscribed to AIER's personal investment service, they departed with a revised portfolio, a more appropriate insurance coverage plan and a few free books. Many offered a check of support for AIER, which Harwood graciously accepted on its behalf.

# Chapter 4:

Why Gold, and What Is Sound Commercial Banking?

*[I]n the absence of governments capable of maintaining stable money, private individuals seek to assure it for themselves, hoarding a purchasing power [gold] more stable than that of any other merchandise . . . stable money is one of the last arms that remains at the disposal of the individual to direct his own affairs, whether it be an enterprise or a simple household.*[17] — Charles Rist, deputy governor of the Banque de France, 1951.

As Harwood put it, the use of gold as money and as the basis for the gold standard was not dreamed up by some central planning board. It evolved as a convenient and stable means of exchanging things, storing value and anchoring the money supply and banking system. No one thought ahead of time that the civilized world would need a better way to trade than primitive bartering. People simply began to use gold or other forms of money many centuries ago, and such usage became more intricate over the centuries with the evolution of banking.

*Why Gold?*

There are a number of reasons why gold has been considered a good store of value. Some of the reasons are:

- Most of us find gold to be beautiful and prize it as jewelry.

- It is relatively rare.
- It is chemically stable, doesn't oxidize and is quasi indestructible; almost all of the stock of gold mined over the centuries is still in existence today.
- No one has yet found a cheap way to manufacture it.
- It is easily divisible.
- It is malleable.
- It is relatively practical to store and transport.
- Its purity can be determined relatively easily.
- It has evolved over the centuries as a medium of exchange and as an anchor to the value of paper money.
- It is found in sufficient quantity to serve the purpose of a fractional gold standard, whereby banks hold an established percentage of their capital in the form of gold reserves.

Ancient Egypt and other regions of the Middle East started using gold in coins around 1500 B.C. The Chinese did likewise around 1091 B.C.[18] The Greeks used metal coinage for several centuries B.C. One particular silver piece, the Athenian "owl," lasted over six centuries, outliving the glorious years of Athens.[19] By the 18th century, gold had become the preferred coinage and monetary reserve substance, with silver a close second. The English started an official gold standard in 1717, which helped the nation preserve the purchasing power of its money for over two hundred years. The U.S. went on the gold standard in 1870, and prices were still stable in the country forty years later. By 1900 most of the developed nations of the world based their money on gold. Harwood considered the stability afforded by the gold standard to be a major factor in facilitating the tremendous commercial advances of those times.

Over the ages, coins and other forms of money were supplied sometimes by private parties and sometimes by governments. However, it is important to note that governments or their delegates have not always monopolized the control of the money supply as they do today. Until 1913 in the U.S., private banks alone were responsible for providing the supply of money to the public, based on their own storage of gold and their short-term lending to private commercial customers. The federal government, on the other hand, handled only the actual coinage and the responsibility for standardizing weights and measures including that of coins. Article I Section 8 of the U.S. Constitution states:

> The Congress shall have Power ... To coin Money, regulate the Value thereof, and of foreign Coin, and fix the Standard of Weights and measures.

During the first few decades of its existence, Congress took its constitutional coinage power at its face value and only concerned itself with the minting and selling of coins. Today in the U.S., although technically the Federal Reserve System is a private institution, no one can really deny the interdependent relationship between the governors of the Fed and the branches of our government that appoint them and define their mandate.

*How Did the Gold Standard Work Under the Private-Bank Monetary System?*

Some readers may wonder how something akin to a fixed gold "price" can help to stabilize the money supply. The idea of fixing the price of anything seems counterintuitive, especially to anyone who went through the 1970's. As we spent hours in line to get gas, we experienced firsthand the law of economics that says fixing a price creates shortages. Few economic rules are as consistently tested and verified in real-world experience as this one.

On the surface, a gold standard seems to be the fixing of a price, and therefore a bad thing. But in fact quite the reverse is taking place. The gold standard anchors the exchange value of a paper money unit that has no intrinsic value to a specified weight of gold that does. And here is the essential point: paper money is not a good like gasoline. It is a promise to pay, like a contract.

A monetary unit—such as the U.S. greenback dollar, the paper English pound, or their bank account equivalent represented by checking accounts or computerized credit balances—is a means of exchange and nothing more. And the fixed price of the monetary unit in terms of gold, or of gold in terms of the monetary unit, is not so much a price in this context as it is a purchasing-value guarantee (gold's purchasing value) behind a contract (the monetary unit). (Please note that the misleading use of the word "price" in this reference to gold under a gold standard is a perfect illustration of why Dewey and Bentley's insistence on precise language is important, and why its absence leads to confusion.)

To insure that each monetary unit retained its value as a specific weight of gold, the gold standard mandated that the banks must accept paper money in exchange for real gold at any time and at a specific rate. Hence, bankers had to maintain sufficient gold reserves in storage to cover any such demand. If the public lost confidence in a bank's capacity to furnish gold in exchange for paper money, they might rush to be the first claimant and cause a panicky run on the bank's gold reserves, as actually happened on numerous occasions. The public, in essence, behaved as the watchdog over the behavior of banks.

Harwood gave at least two examples that illustrate how the gold standard managed to stabilize credit, the price level and whole economies. Both have to do with pricing information signals.

*Example 1*:

Under an international gold standard, countries traded among themselves, and each importer paid for goods with checks exchanged through his international banker. At regular intervals, the various countries' international banking institutions settled up the collective accounts, and the debtor nations shipped either gold itself or claims on gold to their creditor partners. Much of the process was based on faith that the other countries had proper gold backing to their currency, that their banking community's judgment was sound and that no excess credit in the form of money had been issued.

During periods of growth, even under a gold standard, bankers tend to be optimistic. This can lead to excessive lending on risky grounds, which puts too much credit into circulation in the form of money supply. The result has often been a rise in general prices or in the prices of particular assets like real estate or the stock market. The phrase economists use is: "Too much money is chasing too few goods." Harwood termed this process "inflating."

He chose to use the word inflating because the word inflation had lost its precise meaning through sloppy usage. Inflation has come to refer to a rise in the general price level, even though it is defined in some dictionaries as the over-expansion of the money supply that *underlies* the rise in the general price level.

If one country started down the inflationary road and built up more paper money than its reserves and current production could sustain (evidenced, for example, in rising prices), its trading partners would begin to claim physical gold instead of holding the country's gold certificates. This forced the debtor banks to take gold out of their bank vaults and ship it to the creditor nations. The loss of gold reserves was a signal to debtor banks that they should restrain credit creation. This then reduced the amount of money in circulation and eventually rebalanced prices.

*Example 2*:

When over-confident inflating began to occur in a nation under a gold standard, at some point the rising general price level started to cause increased costs for gold production. As a result, gold producers reduced production in the less efficient mines. Meantime, the banks were required at all times to offer gold for a specific exchange value relative to currency. This meant that buyers of gold could turn to the banks for their supply rather than to the gold producers. Again, this reduced banking reserves and encouraged bankers to withdraw credit, thereby rebalancing the money supply and credit.

Harwood's view was that during the decades under the gold standard, money was stable over the longer term. Although the system was not perfect, people around the globe readily accepted payment in gold, gold certificates or gold- or bank-backed paper. Anyone could buy and sell gold coins and bullion on the open market without taxes or penalties, and the legal system defined gold as legal tender.* Currently, gold is not an official form of legal tender, so the public has no choice but to offer what sellers will take, which is usually fiat currency for most transactions. In the U.S. today, the official currency is composed of Federal Reserve notes, U.S. coins and bank accounts that are not backed by much of anything except government debt.

Someone might raise a question about the instability of today's price of gold. In a *Reason* magazine interview, Harwood explained, "Well, of course, the thing that's unstable is the paper money." In times of crisis, whether during ancient wars and recessions or during today's conflicts in the Middle East and economic stress, people will tend to distrust paper in favor of something of known and predictable value. As he said:

> They want to get into something that will be stable when the excitement is over.[20]

---

* Legal tender: "Money that may be legally offered in payment of an obligation and that a creditor must accept." [Webster's New World College Dictionary, 4th ed.] For the most current law, see the U.S. Code, Title 31, Subtitle IV, Chapter 51, Subchapter 1, Section 5103:

> United States coins and currency (including Federal reserve notes and circulating notes of Federal reserve banks and national banks) are legal tender for all debts, public charges, taxes, and dues. Foreign gold or silver coins are not legal tender for debts.

*The Second Part of the Equation: a Sound Commercial Banking System*

In more recent times, after the Civil War in America and at parallel moments in European history, industrial production exploded, multiplying some 50 times over. As critics of the gold standard sometimes note, there wasn't enough gold in the world to supply traders with hard money. To compensate for this shortfall, Harwood explained, a kind of grass-roots system of "real-bills" banking simply evolved. This was a system whereby bankers began to grant short-term credit accounts based not on gold, but on an estimate of the gold-equivalency of the items their clients would produce. To cover gold demand, bankers held a percentage, or fraction, of these transactions as gold reserves in their vault (hence the term "fractional reserve banking").

The bankers did so on the understanding that the credit would be replaced by actual newly-created things coming to market, and that the credit would be fully repaid within a specified short period of time. Thus was needed flexibility added to the rigid gold-based system. As Harwood put it, no economist "had the wit" to invent such a method of handling all the interrelated transactions that were going on, nationally and internationally. It simply evolved. Harwood called it "sound commercial banking," and it helped the gold standard to stabilize the business cycle. Its overall principles were:

- The separation of commercial banking from investment banking, as became codified in the Glass-Steagall Act of 1933 (unfortunately, repealed by the Gramm-Leach-Bliley Act of 1999);
- The maintenance of reasonable gold reserves;
- Conservative lending based only on gold reserves and precise calculations of production and savings; and
- Commercial-bank creation of all money (or purchasing media as Harwood preferred to call it) over and above the gold coins and certificates, the quantity of which was based exclusively on self-

liquidating, short-term commercial transactions collateralized by the gold-exchange value of things coming to market as documented by bills of lading and similar security.

In his books, Harwood often described money as a kind of claim check on someone's share of work product.  In the chain of events as they occurred under the above-described custom of commercial banking, a producer would devise a plan to produce something he thought would be of value to others.  If he had no access to personal savings, he went to his banker for a credit advance against the sales value of the items to be produced. This advance would be used to invest in the raw materials and labor needed.  If the request was accepted, then the banker created the credit and deposited it into the producer's checking account. The items were then produced using the credit to pay for labor and materials. In this fashion, the producer essentially distributed shares of the production to those who had helped to produce it.

Once the goods were sent out in the marketplace and were sold to all those holding claim checks, the money raised by the producer was used to pay off the banker's credit advance.  The loan disappeared off the books, in effect self-liquidating.  The circle was thus complete.  In such a sound money system, every dollar of created credit represented a participant's share of something produced.  None was created that represented nothing.

Bankers could always make mistakes in their lending. However, the gold standard maintained discipline because every banker was required to hold enough gold reserves for any customer who wished to exchange money (claim checks) for gold at the defined rate.  This meant that any errors in a banker's judgment had to be absorbed by the bank's own capital.  The resultant interplay of banking expertise, responsibility to customers and risk of loss was the collective force that controlled the capacity of banks to supply money.

Although not perfect—after all, bankers and their customers are only human—the system worked quite well for extended periods of time, at least from an historical perspective. No team of economists can assure the kind of relative stability experienced for decades by a number of nations under a properly observed gold standard and under a well-run commercial banking system, not even today's sophisticated Federal Reserve governors.

*The Federal Reserve System and "Controlled" Inflating*

With the creation of the Federal Reserve System in 1913, Congress established the structure that would eventually lead to centralized control of the money creation process in the United States. Harwood argued that over time, the Federal Reserve's Board of Governors instigated a policy of chronic inflating based on the advice of eminent economists.

He explained that centrally-driven inflating began to occur in several new ways by the 1940's. First is the direct monetization of government debt, whereby the Federal Reserve Bank creates credit to pay for government deficit spending. As long as the government bonds, bills or notes remain in Fed custody, the Fed-created money dilutes the money supply and debases the currency, because an unknown quantity of the newly created money is not based on actual production and does not self-liquidate.

Second, under the previous system of sound commercial banking, bankers maintained a specific percentage of gold-based reserves relative to their portfolio of short-term commercial loans, savings and other accounts. But in 1933, once Roosevelt declared the holding of gold to be illegal, banks no longer needed to have gold on hand to convert currency into gold on demand. Furthermore, under the new Federal Reserve System, bankers were allowed to hold a part of their reserves in the form of government debt instruments, alongside gold and gold certificates. But as stated earlier, reserves of government debt are sometimes financed by inflationary purchasing media created by the Fed. Together, these new conditions loosened the bankers' control of inflating by removing their incentives to curtail money and credit production.

In this looser monetary environment, bankers began to expand their operations in more precarious ways. One was to lend bank-created credit for things like mortgages, personal loans and stock market operations. Under the previous system of sound commercial banking, all credit creation was limited to short-term commercial operations while the more risky personal lending was financed by actual savings held by the bank.

Lastly, with the evolution of government-regulated banking, bank failures were replaced by centrally-organized takeovers and publicly-financed insurance. This may sound positive, but one forgets that bank failures used to correct the over expansion of bank created money. These corrections no longer occur. Furthermore, as a result of the takeovers, a few banks today have grown to gargantuan size, which has led to the now-familiar issue of banks being too big to fail. The new system replaced healthy and manageable creative destruction with the much more globally destructive moral hazard.

In the light of these observations, why did the economic academics come up with the theory that the Fed should maintain a constantly rising price level through managed chronic inflating? They did so purportedly to smooth out business cycles while giving Congress an instrument to finance what it considered to be necessary and urgent expenses, such as the two world wars. However, as Harwood explained in an interview in *Silver & Gold Report*:

> Inflating allows politicians to spend more than the government takes in without raising taxes.... In short, inflating buys votes and gets you elected. Keynes himself supplied an epilogue: "In the long run we'll all be dead." So why should politicians worry about the end result? ... I think it's theft.[21]

Harwood saw no benefit from such a policy. On the contrary, he saw only the tremendous distortions this macro-management of the money supply would create:

> Big government has grown bigger on the strength of it. Countless bureaucracies and government spending programs materialized as a result of it. Some sharp speculators have gained by it. It has enabled politicians to be reelected to office, so I suppose you can say they've gained by it.

He lamented the lack of education that allows the perpetration of this subtle injustice:

> Somewhere under 5 percent [of the American public], I should imagine, have any real understanding of it. Perhaps only 1 percent has enough understanding to do something effective about it. Considering the magnitude of the theft involved and its duration, one would think the American people would wake up, but surprisingly, they don't.[22]

What is so harmful about rising prices assuming that everyone is aware of the upward creep of the Consumer Price Index (CPI) and everything moves in tandem, for example, salaries, rents, dividends and long-term contracts? The answer is that they don't move in tandem. Harwood's research showed that the CPI adjustments fail to insure everyone against the harms of inflating. During the inflating process, according to his thinking, two things happen that are most unfair to those who are the least prepared to defend themselves.

The first is that when there is chronic inflating, wages, salaries, interest on savings, private pensions, Social Security benefits, Medicare benefits, private life insurance benefits and other income sources of a majority of people do not necessarily increase at the same speed as everyday prices do. For example, during inflationary times an employee might receive raises corresponding more or less to the CPI, but he or she may not think —or dare—to ask for compensation above and beyond the CPI increases for increased productivity. Recent work at AIER has demonstrated that the CPI does not reflect the real inflationary damage on the pocketbook of most consumers.

Well-organized groups, such as unions, can sometimes obtain better deals. As an illustration, in 2011 *USA Today* carried out an analysis of public and private salaries for the same job function using figures published by the Bureau of Labor Statistics. They found a difference of around 12 percent in favor of public workers, without even taking benefits into account. The average wage figures are $67,691 versus $60,046 (2008 numbers). According to the Bureau of Economic Analysis, the public worker received an average of $40,785 worth of benefits, compared to $9,882 for the private worker. Adding the benefits to the salaries raises the difference to 35 percent.[23] These gains come at the expense of the general public who pay more taxes to finance these relatively better compensated public workers.

Another injustice Harwood saw in the inflating process is that the excess money supply in circulation during inflationary episodes alters market perceptions to the point where businesspeople misallocate capital. For example, stock-market or other asset speculation during a rapid boom sometimes promises more profits than creation of a product or service. This happened before the Great Depression of 1929 on Wall Street and in the Florida and New York building booms. During these episodes, many speculators got rich and then went broke, resulting in a tremendous waste of time and energy.

Likewise, during the boom period before the recession of 2007-8, mortgage brokers, builders and Wall Street feasted on low-cost and easily obtained credit. When the bust came, the mortgage brokers and builders went belly up. The large speculating investment banks were so big that Congress voted to bail them out at taxpayer expense.

Even Keynes and Harwood agreed on the ills of inflating.  Keynes wrote:

> By a continuous process of inflation [i.e. inflating], governments can confiscate, secretly and unobserved, an important part of the wealth of their citizens.  By this method, they not only confiscate, but they confiscate arbitrarily; and while the process impoverishes many, it actually enriches some.[24]

# Chapter 5:

Gold as a Hedge Against Devaluation

Harwood first mentioned his interest in protecting investors against a second eventual devaluation of the dollar in two 1944 memos he wrote from his wartime station in the Philippines. They were addressed to Helen and to his statistician, Mr. Ferguson, in Cambridge:

> There is not the slightest doubt that the country will go through a protracted period of severe inflating, probably including some more devaluation.[25] Go ahead and use the copy you prepared re gold and prices etc. for the Research Reports.[26]

During the war the country had gone through a long period of government controls on everything from production requirements to general prices to rationing. The Economists' National Committee on Monetary Policy (ENCMP), of which Harwood was a member, was among the first to warn the nation against continuing these centralized policies during peacetime. One of its members wrote:

> The continuation of the wartime controls of our economy ... is directly inimical and contrary to the traditional "American way of life" for which this terrible war is being fought. We can win the war and win the peace, but may unwittingly lose our very soul.[27]

The Second World War had been financed through some inflating, but Harwood could see from his statistics that Americans had amassed real savings during the stagnation and war years.  He predicted a natural economic expansion as men came home to their jobs and, at last, to a growing economy.  Keynesian economists, however, under-predicted growth, and so instead of allowing the real wealth to pull the economy forward, the Federal Reserve continued inflating, probably fearing another recession like the one after World War I.  As the wars in Europe and Asia cooled, the battle between the Keynesians and the sound-money economists, including Harwood, heated up.

The experts chose their sides.  Marriner S. Eccles, chairman of the Board of Governors of the Federal Reserve System, showed astounding ignorance about the value of gold as a reserve for the banking system when he spoke before Congress.  He called the notion of gold reserves archaic, said that gold was not necessary in the U.S. monetary system and that such restrictions were an imposition.  He pointed out that everyone else—the British, the Canadians, the French and others—had eliminated the gold reserve requirement.  His argument rested upon pure faith that the word of the U.S. government was all that was necessary to shore up the dollar.  "Why have any collateral back of that?" he queried.[28]  The ENCMP, Harwood, and others fought back with articles, Congressional appearances and speeches against these anti-gold notions, but Congress and even some academics were on the side of Eccles.

In an amazingly short period of time, the role of gold in the monetary system disappeared from public consciousness.  As early as 1948, few congressmen were even aware of the workings of a gold standard.  One exception was Representative Howard Buffett, the father of Warren.  Representative Buffett wrote legislation (H.R. 5031), with help from Harwood and the ENCMP, which proposed to return the U.S. to a gold-coin monetary standard and system. However, Buffett lost his bid for reelection, and the bill died alongside his political career. (Just for the anecdote, a younger Howard had lent seed money for Harwood's first AIER project on insurance. In the 1950's son Warren was offered the option of attending educational seminars at AIER, but he preferred to get straight out into the world and do something productive.)

Another representative attempted a gold bill (the Reed Bill, H.R. 3262) in 1949, and again the ENCMP declared its approval and support. This bill also failed to pass. An AIER supporter and industrial businessman, Philip M. McKenna, created the Gold Standard League (GSL). This was an association of gold-standard experts who sought to reignite awareness of gold's monetary role and to clarify the issue for the American public. They hoped to be as successful as the Reform Club Sound Currency Association was in encouraging the Gold Standard Act of 1900.

In 1954, the GSL and the American Economic Foundation (AEF) organized testimony before the Senate during hearings about the Gold Redemption Act of 1954. At that hearing, Harwood argued that a restoration of gold ownership would allow the citizens of the nation to become the overseers of the monetary system once again, as they had been in the decades previous to the 1930s through their personal relationship with their own banks and bankers. The guarantee of a gold-to-currency ratio is vital to the stability of a society, he said. Indeed:

> No truly wise monetary authority or fiscal policy maker should wish to be without such an important guide to policy any more than a sensible automobile driver would discard the speedometer and brakes.[29]

But the wisdom of GSL and AEF did not find favor with the people's representatives in Congress.

Harwood was not surprised.  He no longer had any faith in politicians, especially after Roosevelt's about-face.  Harwood once wrote that "[p]oliticians ... are a different breed of cat," and that much more abuse of the public was going to occur before things changed:

> When times get bad enough, we probably shall get some statesmen, but in the meantime one should not expect forthright and strong leadership until the public's desires are more clearly evident.  Presumably this will not be until more has been embezzled than the $160 billion already taken from life insurance, savings bonds, etc.[30]

Seeing the unnecessary and dangerous inflating but powerless to stop it, Harwood and the AIER faculty did the only thing they could, which was to expose it in the weekly bulletins.  At the same time, knowing the political process pretty well, they also continued guiding investors in the stock market and did splendidly for the next ten years.

With the expansion of AIER and the hiring of personnel, Harwood felt that he could take some much deserved vacation time.  The six family members began traveling in a secondhand Cadillac funeral limousine.  The first trips were weekly summer jaunts down to a beach in Rhode Island, spring drives for Florida sunburns, and visits to family in different parts of the country.  By 1957, they had seen all the National Parks and toured around the 48 states in various generations of the limousine.

Their curiosity about Switzerland and its beautiful Alps took them to Europe.  In Paris, the French franc was going through hard times and losing value by the day.  Men approached Harwood on the street offering to exchange francs for dollars at an advantageous rate.  He was not used to dealing on the black market, but he was tempted.  One evening, he packed his Army-issued .45, which he took along on all trips in those days, and told the boys to stand watch not far away on the street corner in case something went wrong.  He was pretty sure that the Frenchmen were not criminals but simply ordinary citizens with the good sense not to hold onto devaluing paper money. His hopes were confirmed, and everything went without a hitch. To honor the wise French custom of hiding stronger currency and gold pieces under the mattress, Harwood decided to entitle an upcoming article, "Are You as Smart as a French Peasant?"

Harwood had always admired Switzerland because it was one of the few countries with a constitution similar to that of the U.S. It has a strong representative democracy, great respect for minorities and a democratic referendum process. Switzerland also has a modest and unobtrusive presidency, quite unlike the three-ring circus in America. Harwood was charmed by the country's beauty, and he especially liked the people's obvious inclination towards order, punctuality and cleanliness.

He wondered at times if Switzerland wasn't even better suited to enjoy liberty than the U.S. In later years he decided to start a unique university of the social sciences there, one that would be founded on good scientific methodology as he defined it. He began planning such a school in the early 1960's and eventually set out to build it in the canton of Ticino in the Italian part of Switzerland.

He created a Swiss nonprofit called the Progress Foundation to oversee development of the proposed university. He appealed for and received the backing of American investors and the approval of the Swiss government, and he built its first living-quarters project, Falcieu, on a mountaintop in Ciona di Carona that overlooks Lake Lugano. The building is still there, although he died before the university project could make it to completion.

In 1959, two years after the European trip, the family made the long trek in the other direction to Hawaii. As usual, these trips were not simple rest and recreation. Harwood loved to meet people, share ideas and start new projects. On the way back from the trip to Hawaii, he steered the family to Seattle to meet two sociologists who agreed with him about the application of scientific methodology in the social sciences. They were professors George A. Lundberg and Stuart C. Dodd, both at the University of Washington. Lundberg had met and studied with both Dewey and Bentley while at Columbia University.

Soon after Harwood's return home, he began an intense exchange of correspondence with Lundberg and Dodd. They became great friends and founded a nonprofit entity they called the Behavioral Research Council (BRC) to promulgate proper methodology in the social sciences. Harwood was the major force behind it and housed BRC at AIER for the ensuing years. BRC published such studies as *Useful Procedures of Inquiry*, *The Behavioral Sciences: Essays in Honor of George A. Lundberg*, and *A Current Appraisal of the Behavioral Sciences*, plus articles and short booklets. From the outset, BRC sponsored an educational program for young economists to teach them to think more like good scientists.

Institute Staff in the early 1960's

By the late 1950's, AIER's research, investment, secretarial and maintenance departments expanded to about 60 employees. Harwood was writing dozens of articles and a number of booklets every year, aided by his staff. Two works were entitled *Useful Economics* and *Reconstruction of Economics*, in which he attempted to right the skewed vocabulary of the economic science and rectify some of its unsound analytical foundations. The institute's success permitted Harwood to add an annex and a library to the Edgewood plant facilities.

Just as Harwood had predicted, the country's continuing inflationary policies had begun to create exaggerated profits, misallocations, and a serious international balance-of-payments problem. He and his researchers could see it building in their statistics. They blasted the news in their weekly publications and books. They even took out full-page newspaper ads to warn the public and, hopefully, perhaps a few policymakers.

It was still illegal for Americans to hold gold except for coins that were designated as numismatic, so in effect paper money was irredeemable. This meant that the nation was on what ENCMP Professor Walter Spahr called a hybrid standard, where no gold circulated in the U.S. but where all trading nations used a bullion gold standard to balance their own accounts. In other words, trading nations could exchange dollars for gold at a rate of $35 an ounce, but America's own citizens could not.

By this time, most western countries had renounced any serious effort to respect the gold standard even though they had been using the commercial London gold market in an official capacity to clear international transactions since 1954. Harwood knew the politicians and the Fed would not rein in inflating. This meant that another devaluation was inevitable. He was so sure of this that he and his staff started recommending legal gold investments in 1958, such as permitted numismatic coins and gold stocks.

In 1959, the market price for gold on the London exchange began to rise above the standard $35 an ounce, which was disquieting to international money managers. A group of countries banded together to form what they called the gold pool. The goal was to control the gold price by the organized selling of large quantities of national reserves of gold. They were unsuccessful. The unofficial exchange rate kept rising, even though after a few years the U.S. had divested itself of 120 tons of its gold stock.

As the situation progressed, Harwood scouted out more exotic but still legal financial products related to gold or foreign assets where the investment clients could preserve their hard-earned savings against the coming devaluation. To Harwood, *not* to have recommended these investments would have been, if not criminal, at least negligent, and would have represented the shirking of both his fiduciary duty to institute clients and his sworn oath to the American people. Harwood saw the inflating of the currency as a flagrant disregard by Congress of its constitutional obligation to preserve the value of the nation's currency. Furthermore, a *de jure* gold standard was still on the books.

In the midst of this, AIER found itself in a skirmish with tax authorities about its nonprofit status. It may have seemed to some that Harwood actually enjoyed these frequent provocations from government agents judging from the number of times he found himself opposite them. However, the reality was that he simply had little tolerance for what he called "peanut authority." He would remain steadfast to his honorable principles no matter what the cost or pain. This time, in a down-to-the-finish compromise with the IRS in 1962, AIER agreed to split off the investment advisory service into a wholly-owned subsidiary. They named it the American Institute Counselors (AIC). This entity took over the investment aspects of AIER's work and solved the nonprofit status problem for AIER.

AIC continued Harwood's initiative of moving client funds into gold-hedged instruments, while AIER concentrated on the theoretical economic and public-policy research and education. Other investment services were also advising moves into gold related assets, enough so that President Eisenhower's advisors noted the trend. The President renewed Roosevelt's restrictions on gold ownership by executive order, declared another state of emergency just before Kennedy took office in January of 1962 and forbade the direct holding of gold abroad.

The trade imbalance got worse. Soon came further legislation to stop a flight from the dollar by discouraging foreign investments. The Kennedy administration imposed a limitation on cash taken out of the country. In 1963, Congress passed the Interest Equalization Tax, a tax on the interest from foreign securities. Harwood recommended that AIC clients pay the tax and that they place foreign investments with bankers outside the country, still permitted under then-current law. He remembered the days when a stroke of Roosevelt's pen nullified the people's property rights in America, and he was confident that eventual profits would be substantial enough to cover any penalties Congress could invent.

An independent foreign supervisory entity began to manage all of the financial instruments for a small annual fee of three-tenths of 1 percent, just enough to cover its own expenses with little to spare. Few, if any, other account managers charged such a low fee. By January of 1966, AIC was advising clients to reduce American common stocks in their portfolios to the lowest level ever recommended since 1934. At the same time, they were to increase the percentage in gold stocks.[31]

More legislation was in the works. Congress passed the Tax Reform Act of 1969 extending the Interest Equalization Tax and making it far more restrictive. AIC bulletins warned clients that the government would try to stem fund outflows by imposing increasingly penalizing rules and regulations. Clients were advised to continue doing whatever was legal to protect their savings.

Another new law forced Americans to declare to the IRS every three months that they and their foreign agents were not investing in foreign stocks simply to avoid the payment of tax. During the next year, Congress added a section to the IRS 1040 tax return form that requires taxpayers to divulge the existence of all foreign bank accounts. For some reason, legislators stopped just short of forbidding foreign investment altogether.

As so often happens, these new legislative restrictions had the opposite of the intended effect. They incited a natural tendency in people to become wary of their own government and to search for more ways to protect their interests from feared or real confiscation. In spite of the tax burdens, investors in gold and foreign assets were going to receive an excellent return, and they knew it. But just in case, Harwood decided to send out a bulletin explaining the dangers of the situation and giving all AIC investors the chance to withdraw their funds, even from some irrevocable trusts. Only a few withdrew.

By the early 1970's, the country found itself faced with the inevitable buildup of foreign claims on U.S. dollars that couldn't be paid at the declared gold exchange rate. One infamous day in 1971, President Nixon threw in the monetary towel by walking away from our foreign creditors, as Roosevelt had done before him. The gold standard was declared officially dead three years later. The dollar was worth about one-fourth of its 1913 purchasing power, which meant that anyone still holding fixed-dollar instruments over this time period—checking and savings accounts, life insurance, long-term treasury bonds, foreign dollar holdings—found themselves "embezzled" out of up to three-quarters of their investments' purchasing power.

As a gold bull market became a sure thing, AIC recommended that investors who were not retired put all their extra savings into gold coins plus gold stocks, keeping an appropriate amount of cash reserves according to their personal circumstances.[32] Small civil rights groups began to organize around the country protesting the new restrictive laws.

Then, in what may seem a surprising move after the official abandonment of the gold standard in December 1973, Congress loosened the restrictions on American ownership of rare and unusual gold coins minted from 1934 through 1959. The next year, on December 31, 1974, Public Law 93-373 made it legal to own any gold coins. Finally, President Ford's Executive Order 11825 of the same date revoked all previous orders pertaining to limitation of gold ownership.

The legal changes regarding gold ownership were, at least in part, due to the efforts of Harwood, the ENCMP and other entities. They were also due to the extraordinary energy of brave individuals such as Jim Blanchard III. Blanchard and his associate Evan Soulé had formed the National Committee to Legalize Gold in 1971. To make their point, they flew a small plane around the capital during the Nixon inauguration with a banner reading, "Legalize Gold." However, their victory was only partial.

The gold standard may have been dead and gold ownership finally liberated, but there was a hitch: gold was now declared to be a commodity like any other and therefore subject to capital gains and sales tax. This has the effect of confiscating a significant percentage of the value at every retail transaction. Perhaps members of Congress thought that the abandonment of the gold standard, combined with these tax measures, would put an end to gold hoarding and speculation. In reality, investors turned to it even more over the following decade. Relieved of its official gold standard mantle, gold embarked on a four-year speculative frenzy as the overvalued dollar found its new level of exchange. As economist Alan Reynolds once put it, "People never leave the gold standard—only governments do."[33]

# Chapter 6: The Last Act

*Under the guise of "protective" law, Congress has created a fourth branch of government … a maze of regulatory agencies which are variously estimated to cost the American consumer $150 billion a year [$613 billion in 2013 dollars]. These agencies are accountable to no one, and since they both interpret and administer their own pronouncements, they wield the power to wound or kill whole industries. The cost is higher prices, lost jobs, increased taxes. Evaporating investment is cheap, however, compared to the price we pay in lost freedom.* -- Attributed to Gerald H. Trautman, Chairman of the Board of the Greyhound Corporation, 1976.[34]

By his early 70's Harwood was starting to feel his age. He thought he detected a heart attack, although the doctors couldn't confirm it. At the same time, he was becoming something of a celebrity in the financial press. One of the more visible pieces was a May 1973 front-page article in *The Wall Street Journal* entitled "Mr. Gloom & Doom." It had the subtitle:

How a Pessimist Makes His Clients Rich in Gold by Predicting Disaster. Harwood Sees Depression Worse Than in '29, Thinks Even Bonds and Land Risky. Mr. Diamond [an AIC client] Turns to Gold.[35]

The article was a long piece describing Harwood as an eccentric. It cited his Index of Inflating and AIC's recommendations for investing in gold and gold stocks. More articles appeared in *The Wall Street Journal, Time* and elsewhere, treating Harwood, AIER and AIC as butts of gold-bug jokes. However, as the London gold price climbed, the financial press began to change its tone.

Perhaps it was AIER's newfound notoriety, or maybe it was Harwood's public reference to the SEC as the "Swindlers' Encouragement Commission." For whatever reason, the SEC also began to turn its eye to the institute. Harwood did not expect any attention from this particular agency in spite of his repeated public expressions of disdain for federal bureaucracies. His lack of wariness is surprising given his experience with the genre. He must have been relying on the facts that AIER and AIC were both in compliance with all the government agencies, and that they had sent every bulletin to the SEC since AIER registered its investment advisory service in the 1930's. The Commission's silence over the years was interpreted to mean it had no objection to the investment activities.

What followed could have been a very dark moment in Harwood's life, but it turned out to be one of his brightest. SEC agents began an 18-month investigation in May of 1974. At first, they may have thought that Harwood was a typical Ponzi-scheme swindler with expensive tastes and hidden million-dollar yachts off the coast of Monte Carlo, all at his investors' expense. To their surprise, they located him living openly in a modest rental apartment in Europe with no security gates or armed bodyguards.

While the SEC investigated AIER and AIC's activities over a period of months, the researchers continued to publish articles on erroneous public and monetary policy. One typical report in July 1975 cited the removal of the gold reserve requirement behind the dollar as the last barrier to chronic inflating. The report also declared that the buying power of the dollar was now in the hands of a few inflationist money-credit managers who were more worried about escaping a depression—that they themselves would cause—than in reducing inflating. Unsound businesses and margin speculators had found capital during the credit boom, and private citizens had expanded their own balance sheets to an untenable degree. AIC saw no hope for a normal cyclical recovery and continued to advise all clients to place their disposable funds abroad in foreign and gold-related instruments, paying any taxes that might be required.

> Those who would demonetize gold in order to facilitate their embezzlement of private wealth and maintain their positions of power in governments and central banks are following policies that must inevitably teach every intelligent citizen the usefulness of gold.[36]

The words were premonitory. However, the SEC didn't see it this way. To these government agents, such inflammatory language must have seemed like outright heresy.

While the investigation was going on, the political battle in the U.S. to suppress foreign investment was growing. Legislators enacted more tax laws in an effort to close in on the fight of capital to foreign shores. As Harwood noted, Congressional leaders may have thought they were curing a balance-of-payment problem, but what they were doing in effect was attempting to force Americans to shoulder the loss from the upcoming devaluation. At no time did Congress see that those who had over-inflated the money supply were responsible for causing these losses, and that the public they represented was about to become the victim.

In September 1976, just as President Ford signed yet another tax reform act into law reducing some of the benefits of foreign trusts and imposing more new taxes, Jesse Helms submitted a gold clause amendment to Congress. It was a proposal for the reinstatement of gold as a potential medium for contractual arrangements. Writers of support letters published in the Congressional Record of September 1976 included Nobel Prizewinning economist Milton Friedman, Ernie Welker of AIER and Harwood. The clause passed the next year, but it had few teeth given gold's new status as an ordinary taxable commodity.

Harwood continued to recommend gold in a new personal publication he named the *Phoenix Bulletin*. In November 1976 he wrote:

> If there were convincing evidence that the leading industrial nations had decided to return to sound money, i.e. the gold standard, one could forget gold and gold stocks. As yet, however, we see no evidence whatsoever that the governments and money managers have decided to reform. On the contrary, their primary concern seems to be to persuade citizens that paper is better than gold, so that the inflating may be continued indefinitely.[37]

Delays in the SEC matter put AIER and AIC on hold, but they afforded Harwood enough personal free time to prepare not just his new bulletins, but also his last book, *The Money Mirage*. It was ready for circulation in November 1976.

Shortly thereafter, Harwood's writings began to take a turn toward a wider, more somber philosophical perspective, coinciding with the discovery that he needed a prostate operation. In the June 1977 *Phoenix* he wrote about America's great principles of human rights and justice that came to be embodied in the U.S. Constitution. Those principles include strict limitation of power and function at the highest level of government, without which we drift away from freedom "into the hands of interventionist bureaucrats."

> Liberty is ... an essential ingredient of a just and lasting social order. Many years ago, I took an oath, "to preserve and defend the Constitution of the United States against all its enemies, foreign and domestic." I confess that then the significance of that oath in my mind was concerned primarily with World War I. However, through a fortunate series of accidents and intellectual curiosity I have found in that oath far more significance. It has become my guiding star and I

hope my children and grandchildren will make it theirs. It is the light of that star that gleams at the end of the tunnel.

Now I feel that I should apologize for almost preaching to you. I had intended only to share with you some of the lessons learned and conclusions developed during a half century of work in the field of economic and social problems.[38]

In another *Phoenix*, he wrote about the "Golden Opportunity" laying ahead for those who were wise enough to understand the process of inflating. He saw no reason to hope that "the life cycle of the inflating-embezzling-enslaving syndrome" had to be less than several decades long. He cited the case of France, where the process was ongoing since 1914. He predicted that the United States would achieve a crushing burden of debt that would likely create social disorder within the next 40 to 60 years.

He described the unholy alliances among the leading politicians, the central bankers and other leading bankers, all of whom would work together to maintain the credibility of paper money so the inflating could continue. They will denigrate gold and attempt to suppress the gold price as long as possible. But, he wrote, gold is the "key to freedom, ... the implacable enemy of unredeemable paper," and they will fail in the long run because gold will always appreciate in terms of depreciating paper currencies. "Once again, freedom and gold will be found to be inseparable."[39] Gold was exchanging at about $160 an ounce at the time.

During the late 1970's, the political climate in the U.S. relative to gold continued to improve. In October 1977, a year after Helms presented his gold clause amendment allowing contracts to specify payment in gold or gold-value equivalent, President Carter signed it into law. Unfortunately, the Treasury Department took the clearly cynical position that:

[I]n the light of demonstrated volatility in the price of gold that makes widespread use of gold as a measure of value in private transactions unlikely … [the repeal of gold restrictions] would not have undesirable monetary effects. The Treasury Department therefore supports such repeal as an appropriate step in treating gold like other commodities.[40]

In other words, Treasury authorities presumed citizens would make little use of this gold-clause option, and therefore the legislation would neither cause a flight from the dollar nor inhibit the Federal Reserve's capacity to manipulate the money supply or the dollar's purchasing power. This assessment was accurate, given the unfavorable tax treatment of retail gold transactions and the volatility of gold's price relative to the dollar. However, even if only as a symbol, the legal change was welcomed by those who believed in freedom.

After four years and with the help of some excellent legal work, Harwood and the more stalwart investors survived the fight against the SEC. The agency eventually dropped the lawsuit leaving the investments intact. Even the long delays caused by the auditors and courts worked in the investors' favor as gold, and hence the value of the portfolios, climbed to new heights.

At a celebratory cocktail party, John D. Aldock, one of the institute's new Washington lawyers, reportedly said to Harwood, "Ed, it's too bad you didn't consult with us a long time ago. We could have saved you a lot of grief." Harwood's reply was, "On the contrary, I'm glad we never met. You wouldn't have let me do it."

Gold soon zipped through $200 an ounce and never looked back. It even hit a high of $800 an ounce, albeit only temporarily, as the dollar once again sought its real level at an all-time low. Today, although the metal's price instability and penalizing tax treatment have indeed rendered it unpopular as a medium of contractual exchange, it has managed to climb to $1,900 in 2012. This means, of course, that the value of paper currencies has never been so feeble and insecure, and for good reason, since the inflating process has not stopped to this day.

Harwood gave a bitter argument against the SEC's very existence in an interview with *Reason* magazine:

> [Harwood:] [The SEC] is worse than nothing. I'll tell you why it's worse than nothing. It has facilitated tremendous losses for investors by the red herring. You know what the red herring is? Any firm that wants to sell securities has to get out this voluminous documentation, but there's red print on the front of it indicating that the SEC has not approved it. Any investor confronted with all that paperwork thinks, "Well, of course, maybe they haven't approved it, but what are they there for but to protect me? Why do they exist if not to protect me?" So he assumes that somehow they're protecting him. [41]

In other words, as Harwood so often said, there really is no substitute for integrity. Honest people will never purposely mislead for personal gain, whereas the dishonest ones will always find a way to turn even the most sophisticated hurdles to their advantage.

Can any government watchdog fulfill the purpose it was intended to fulfill? The record is bleak. Harwood said in an internal memo:

> In my opinion ... the danger to the United States arises from the very nature of such agencies as the SEC, dangers that our founding fathers foresaw so well. Inevitably attracted to such jobs are the dedicated interventionists, the meddling busybodies who are so sure that they can manage the lives of their fellow citizens better than the citizens can. The historical record demonstrates that few men are more dangerous than those convinced of their own righteousness who have been given inordinate power over their fellow citizens. [42]

In an AIER piece entitled "View from an Alp" he wrote:

[A]s I endeavor, on this Alpine vantage point to see as clearly as I can, I am inclined to wonder. If there is a just God and a Recording Angel, whom will be assigned the greater blame? Will it fall on the men, simple human beings like us all, who were induced, perhaps seduced, to climb into the seats of power where power corrupted them, or will much of the blame fall on those who in their eager efforts to mind their neighbors' business created the Government agencies and bureaucracies where the corruptible power seekers flourish? In any event, were not our forefathers exceedingly wise when they sought to create and maintain Government at the highest level with strictly limited powers?[43]

\*　　　\*　　　\*　　　\*　　　\*

The surprisingly positive ending of the SEC case brought notoriety to Harwood. Most of the SEC's probes were catastrophic for those charged, whether the investigated party was guilty or innocent. But Harwood, the institute and the braver investors, representing some 85 percent of them, had weathered the storm and come out ahead of the game. He began to receive standing ovations wherever he spoke. One gold bug group minted a one ounce gold piece with his likeness. He was the first of three to be so honored, the second being von Hayek and the third Henry Hazlitt—excellent company indeed. Typical of Harwood, he insisted that the coin not bear his name, but instead the words "American Institute for Economic Research" and "For integrity there is no substitute."

As he explained to a reporter from the *Silver & Gold Report,* more of the American people needed to wake up and stop investing in the usual assets—life insurance, savings and the bond and stock markets—and start putting their cash into something that could not be depreciated by government design. He imagined several possible scenarios for the upcoming crisis he saw on the horizon. One possibility was a deflationary crash that put an end to it all, with "snowballing bankruptcies that would be too great for the Washington printing presses to cope with." A second scenario was hyperinflation as occurred in post-World War I Germany. But the most likely, he felt, was this:

> [W]e're more apt to be surprised the other way in that the presses that print the currency and government bonds that are stuffed into the Federal Reserve will run at whatever speed required to keep the bubble from collapsing. As long as the government is willing to issue more inflationary purchasing media, I imagine the politicians and money managers can keep the song and dance going right along, perhaps for decades.[44]

In other interviews and speeches, he argued that civilizations that milked their citizens by depreciating the currency have tended to collapse. He advised Americans to buy gold instead of the usual assets, not only as a safer and perhaps more profitable investment in the longer run, but also to communicate dissatisfaction with chronic inflating and to force a "re-evolution" of a proper monetary standard.[45] The world didn't have to go back to the gold standard *per se*. It should allow itself to go *forward* to something resembling a modernized gold standard, within the context of a sounder system of commercial banking that is kept separate from investment banking.

Events on the ground proved him right. For example, just as the Western World was thinking it had left the gold standard behind, President Carter signed a bill allowing the U.S. Treasury to sell 300,000 ounces of gold per month. The U.S. government was apparently still convinced it could stop the national currency's relentless decline through such manipulations. Harwood heralded the desperate measure as the beginning of a return to gold. It signaled to him that gold was still a major actor in world economics:

> As the paper money managers most loudly proclaim their determination to abandon gold, they reach for the golden life preserver to keep their paper afloat, apparently without conscious recognition of the fact that they have begun the return to the gold standard. Thus they demonstrate once again the absurdity of their irrationality.[46]

It seems you can take gold out of the standard, but you can't take the standard out of gold.

Harwood opined that some form of gold reference would inevitably appear down the line. "No doubt, the road will be long and rocky, quite different from the smooth slide of inflating."[47] In a letter to friend John Exter, he wrote:

> Perhaps the ultimate return to the gold standard and monetary health will be a slowly progressing evolutionary type of development beginning here and there and finally accepted on a wider scale as it works in practice. It is too early to visualize details of procedures, but almost surely freedom to contract in terms of and ready availability of gold, perhaps in metric weight units for universal convenience, will be [part of the] solution. Such are my present random thoughts.[48]

*     *     *     *     *

Harwood expressed his life goal most succinctly in a letter to Helen in 1944, just before shipping off to the Pacific war theater:

> Above all else, I want [my children] to understand why the great principles of our Constitution are worth all that men can give.... I

would like them to learn to know and appreciate what has seemed to me worth fighting for, in war and peace. [49]

He knew that he could not carry out this fight alone, that the American people as a group are responsible for maintaining the constitutional limitations on their government. Without these limitations, our unique way of life—indeed freedom itself—is in jeopardy. He knew the power of small outspoken groups of people, which he called "balance-of-power minorities." He believed AIER and AIC's members constituted such vocal minorities in some of their own Congressional districts. Such groups are protected by America's form of government and can direct the future of the nation through collective actions and votes.

He gave the example of the five million farm operations in the U.S. In spite of the fact that only a few thousand of these benefit from America's extensive farm program, it remains in effect due to this small group's pressure on legislators. In fact, he stated, only three so-called "farmers" collect more money from the government than do all the farmers of Delaware, Pennsylvania, and New Jersey.

[P]oliticians have only one deep-seated conviction, that they should be reelected. They are like weather vanes and will turn with the winds of preference indicated by articulate minorities. As for what will happen if an independent minority does not become educated and active, one need not be a prophet to foresee that. The answer has been written in the history books time and again. [50]

Harwood believed that the teaching profession also held a good deal of the responsibility for educating students about the Constitution. On this subject he spoke eloquently to an academic audience at Georgetown University:

I am not enough of a Pollyanna to offer you hope of success if you do what you can to help bring the light of understanding where there now is darkness. But in the last analysis we each must confront one critic, one judge from whom we can conceal nothing and who will decide our merits. I refer to the better aspects of the inner self. Everyone who has not lost his guiding star, the better aspects of his inner self, to every such person I offer the promise that even if we lose in the great attempt to preserve and defend the United States, to restore it as what it once was, the last great hope of mankind; even if we lose that battle, you can at least retain the approval of your inner self if you do what is in your power to do.[51]

*    *    *    *    *

During his last year, 1980, Harwood spoke of his hope for the future. Reagan's campaign was in full swing and the country seemed to be turning towards more sound fiscal principles.

[Reason Magazine:] There have been, over the last few years, what seem to be important shifts—a shift of policy on the Federal Reserve Board toward deciding to get the money supply under control, or at least saying they're going to. There's a new mood of budget balancing in Congress. There's a general tax revolt going on in this country. Are you any more optimistic about the future of this country now than you were, say, five years ago?

[Harwood] If I weren't, I probably would have cut my throat. I think that some of the people are being hurt so much that they're waking up. It's now, I would guess, about two or three years that, in spite of all sorts of increases in wages, people's real incomes have been going down.  And I think that's a very strong inducement to common sense.  It makes you think.  And get enough people thinking, and you can't tell what they'll do.  They may do a wise thing.  And I think they made enough noise, particularly out here in California, so they've got the politicians running scared.  After all, what does a politician want?  He wants his job.  And no politician, no man, no human being, can do what a politician has to do, go around and cultivate all those votes and satisfy all those people, and still know anything about what he's doing.  So what we've got to have, if we're going to be saved, is enough people hollering loudly enough that the politicians react to it.…  I'm always encouraged when I see a little bit of evidence of more people exercising common sense than they seemed to before.[52]

\*    \*    \*    \*    \*

Harwood died on the night of December 16, 1980.  His executor revealed that Harwood had given instructions to mail a small box of his old socks and underwear to the IRS in a last defiant gesture towards the government bureaucrats.

THE END

# Epilogue
## Excerpts from *A Time for Truth* by William E. Simon

Harwood devoted part of one *Phoenix Bulletin* to citations from an excellent book by William E. Simon entitled *A Time for Truth*. Simon was secretary of the treasury for three years, from 1974 to 1977. With the permission of Mr. Simon's heirs, and out of respect for Harwood's deference to the work, the author presents you with a couple of the passages that Harwood found so important:

> During my four years in Washington … Chiefs of State and finance ministers of America's Western allies told me with great concern that they no longer knew how to sustain the levels of economic support which their citizens had come to believe was their "right." All were counting on America to save them….

> [Leaders] have lost the knowledge "born of long ages of suffering under man's dominion over man … that the exercise of unlimited power by men with limited minds and self-regarding prejudices is soon oppressive, reactionary and corrupt." They have lost this knowledge because today— although in their collectivist "idealism" they cannot grasp this—*they* are the reactionary, corrupt oppressors…. The powerful political intelligentsia that determines the trends in social democratic nations today is as stubborn and ruthless a ruling elite as

any in history and worse than many because it is possessed of delusions of moral grandeur…. The *last* thing to do is to fight conventionally in the political arena, on the assumption that getting Republicans or conservatives of both parties into office is a solution…. [I]t solves nothing fundamental…. Similarly, one should not come up with programs of one's own. Not only would they turn out, in the current context, to be modified egalitarian authoritarian programs, but also the very approach is itself a symptom of the interventionist disease. The incessant spawning and modification of laws, regulations, programs, and "national purposes" are the expressions of a state which sees its primary function as a controller of citizens….

The overriding principle to be revived in American political life is that which sets individual liberty as the highest political value—that value to which all other values are subordinate and that which, at all times, is to be given the highest "priority" in policy discussions….

A critical principle which must be communicated forcefully to the American public is the inexorable interdependence of economic wealth and political liberty. Our citizens must learn that what keeps them prosperous is production and technological innovation. Their wealth emerges, not from government offices or politicians' edicts, but only from that portion of the marketplace which is *free*…. Bureaucracies themselves should be assumed to be noxious, authoritarian parasites on society, with a tendency to augment their own size and power and to cultivate a parasitical clientele in all classes of society.[53]

1.  "Col. E.C. Harwood: 'Gold is the primary medium for defense against inflation,'" *Silver & Gold Report* (Newtown, CT:  Early March 1978), pp.5-7.

2.  Brigadier General G.B. Pillsbury, Corps of Engineers, Acting Chief of Engineers, Memo to E.C. Harwood, November 16, 1935.

3.  E.C. Harwood, Memo to the Adjutant General of the Army, Washington, D.C., October 8, 1934.

4.  Brigadier General G.B. Pillsbury, Corps of Engineers, Acting Chief of Engineers, to E.C. Harwood, November 16, 1935.

5.   E.C. Harwood, "Deterioration of the American Banking Portfolio, a Comprehensive Ratio Analysis, 1920 to 1928 Inclusive," *The Annalist* (New York Times: August 2, 1929), p.205, quoted with the kind permission of Bloomberg Legal Department.

6.  Attributed to good friend George Hester.

7.  Einstein's letter to Vivienne Anderson of May 12, 1953, AEA 60-716 in the Einstein archives,  © The Hebrew University of Jerusalem.

8.  D. Everett, *Columbia Orator*, 1777; also, the title of a talk given by second wife Helen after Harwood's death.

9.  E.C. Harwood, Letter to mother, December 19, 1920.

10. E.C. Harwood, Report to Group Members, January 5, 1928.

11. According to www.schmoop.com/fdr-new-deal/ideology.html

12. Quote sent to Rollo Handy by Theodore Brenner of Franklin College, with the note, "I thought you might enjoy this!", June 27, 1983.

13. Excerpt from the Articles of Association of A.I.E.R., June 27, 1939.

14. E.C. Harwood, Letter to George A. Lundberg, June 1, 1961.

15. "Harwood Blames New Deal Economics for Current Trade Slump," *San Francisco Chronicle* (San Francisco: 1938).

16. E.C. Harwood, Memo to Voting Members of AIER, October 14, 1978.

17. Charles Rist, "The Price of Gold in the United States," *L'Opinion*, February 15, 1951, p.138, made available on the web by the Ludwig Von Mises Institute as Charles Rist, *The Triumph of Gold* (New York: Wisdom Library, a division of Philosophical Library, 1961).

18. "The History of Gold," National Mine Association (Washington, D.C.) currently available on the web at: http://www.nma.org/pdf/gold/gold_history.pdf

19. John H. Wood, *Money: Its Origins, Development, Debasement, and Prospects*, an *Economic Education Bulletin* of the American Institute for Economic Research (Great Barrington, MA: 1999), pp.15-17.

20. Reason Interview: "Col. E.C. Harwood," *Reason Magazine* (Los Angeles: June 1981), pp.62-63.

21. "Col. E.C. Harwood: 'Gold is the primary medium for defense against inflation,'" *Silver & Gold Report* (Newtown, CT: Early March 1978), pp.3-4.

22. *Ibid.*

23. Dennis Cauchon, "Federal pay ahead of private industry," *USA Today* (McLean, VA: updated March 8, 2010), web address as of May 30, 2011: http://www.usatoday.com/news/nation/2010-03-04-federal-pay_N.htm

24. John Maynard Keynes, *Economic Consequences of the Peace* (1924), Macmillan Publishers Ltd., reproduced with permission of Palgrave Macmillan.

25. E.C. Harwood, Letter to Helen, approximately December 1943.

26. E.C. Harwood, Memo to Ferguson, March 21, 1944.

27. Ray B. Westerfield, "The Restoration of Free Markets," *The Commercial and Financial Chronicle*, (June 21, 1945).

28. Marriner S. Eccles, spoken before the Committee on Banking and Currency, U.S. Senate on S.510 (February 20, 28 and March 7, 1945), pp.18, 21-22, 29, 34, 47.

29. E.C. Harwood, "Advantages of Returning to the Full Gold Standard with the Nation's Currency Redeemable in Gold Coin on Demand," testimony before the U.S. Senate during hearings on the Gold Redemption Act of 1954, *Special Bulletin*, American Institute for Economic Research (Great Barrington, MA: May 20, 1954), p.2.

30. E.C. Harwood, Letter to Philip McKenna, February 7, 1955.

31. E.C. Harwood, "Who is Guarding the Interests of Investors?" October 11, 1974, self-published and written on AIC letterhead.

32. *Ibid.*

33. Alan Reynolds, "Managed Money," Lecture given at Progress Foundation on April 27, 1984, p.115, published currently on the Foundation's website at: www.progressfoundation.ch/PDF/referate/87_Lecture Alan Reynolds_27.4.1984_E.pdf

34. Gerald H. Trautman, Chairman of the Board of the Greyhound Corporation, quoted by Donald C. Seberg, DDS in a letter to ECH, January 10, 1977.

35. Alfred L. Malabre, Jr., "Mr. Gloom & Doom, How a Pessimist Makes His Clients Rich in Gold by Predicting Disaster," *The Wall Street Journal* (New York: May 30, 1973).

36. "Quarterly Review of Investment Policy," *Investment Bulletin*, American Institute Counselors, Incorporated (Great Barrington, MA: July 21, 1975).

37. *Phoenix Economic Bulletin*, Vol.1, No.11 (Bermuda: Constitutional Liberty Trust, November 1976), p.41.

38. "Sovereign or Slave?", *Phoenix Economic Bulletin*, Vol.II, No.6 (Bermuda: Constitutional Liberty Trust, June 1977), p.24.

39. "Emancipation from Economic Slavery," *Phoenix Economic Bulletin*, Vol.II, No.11 (Bermuda: Constitutional Liberty Trust, November 1977), pp.41-44.

40. U.S. Treasury position paper on S. 79, a bill to restore the freedom to use gold clauses in contacts, quoted in "News Briefs," Gold Standard Corporation (Kansas City: October 1977) p.2.

41. Reason Interview: "Col. E.C. Harwood," *Reason Magazine* (Los Angeles: June 1981), pp.61-62.

42. E.C. Harwood, Memo, "Prepared to Cope With the Worst," American Institute Counselors, Incorporated (Great Barrington, MA: August 12, 1975), p.3.

43. "View From An Alp: Conspiracy," *Economic Education Bulletin*, American Institute for Economic Research (Great Barrington, MA: October 1974), p.3. See, also, selected quotes from William E. Simon's book, *A Time for Truth*, in the Epilogue to this biography.

44. "Col. E.C. Harwood: 'Gold is the primary medium for defense against inflation,'" *Silver & Gold Report* (Newtown, CT: Early March 1978), pp.5-7.

45. E.C. Harwood, "Stop thieves!", an address before the 4th Annual NCMR Conference in Nassau, reprinted in *Phoenix Economic Bulletin* (Constitutional Liberty Trust, June 1978), p.30.

46. "From Gold to Paper and Return," *Phoenix Economic Bulletin*, Vol.III, No.7 (Bermuda: Constitutional Liberty Trust, July 1978), p.33.

47. *Ibid.*

48. E.C. Harwood, Letter to John Exter, February 1, 1963.

49. E.C. Harwood, Letter to Helen dated June 24, 1944, kept with him until he mailed it to himself at the Cambridge address on March 8, 1945, once he knew he was on his way back from the war.

50. E.C. Harwood, Letter to Mr. R.E. Swarthout, March 3, 1960.

51. E.C. Harwood, Speech: "The Suicide of Western Civilization," delivered at a Committee for Monetary Reform and Education conference at Georgetown University, Washington D.C., November 14, 1974, published in *Investment Bulletin*, American Institute Counselors, Incorporated, Vol. XLI No. 23 (Great Barrington, MA: December 2, 1974), p.90.

52. Reason Interview: "Col. E.C. Harwood," *Reason Magazine* (Los Angeles: June 1981), pp.58-63.

53. William E. Simon, *A Time for Truth*, Reader's Digest Press, McGraw-Hill Book Company (New York: 1978). Quoted with the kind permission of William E. Simon, Jr.